The Japanese Invasion of Man‹
of the Most Notorious E\

By Charles River Editors

A picture of Japanese troops marching into Mukden on September 18, 1931

About Charles River Editors

Charles River Editors provides superior editing and original writing services across the digital publishing industry, with the expertise to create digital content for publishers across a vast range of subject matter. In addition to providing original digital content for third party publishers, we also republish civilization's greatest literary works, bringing them to new generations of readers via ebooks.

Sign up here to receive updates about free books as we publish them, and visit Our Kindle Author Page to browse today's free promotions and our most recently published Kindle titles.

Introduction

A picture of Lieutenant General Shigeru Honjō, commander in chief of the Japanese forces in Manchuria, acknowledging the salutes of a procession of Japanese residents of Mukden celebrating the establishment of a new puppet state in Manchuria

The Invasion of Manchuria

"Here, many hundreds of leagues from home,

The red setting sun of distant Manchuria

Shines down on a stone at the edge of a field,

Beneath which my friend lies.

It grieves me to think of the brave hero

Who only yesterday headed the charge –

Ruthlessly setting upon the enemy.

I wonder, will he sleep well here?" - "Senyu," a Japanese song from the Russo-Japanese War,

Though scarcely mentioned in the world of early 21st century politics, Manchuria represented a key region of Asia during the first half of the 20th century. Once the heartland of the fierce Manchu empire, this northeastern Chinese region's rich natural resources made it a prize for nations in the process of entering the modern age, and three ambitious nations in the midst of such a transformation lay close enough to Manchuria to attempt to claim it: Japan, Russia, and China.

For countries attempting to shake off their feudal past and enter a dynamic era of industrialization, Manchuria's resources presented an irresistible lure. With immense natural resources coupled to economic activity more concentrated than elsewhere in China, this region, abutting Mongolia, Korea, the Yellow Sea, and the Great Wall "accounted for 90 percent of China's oil, 70 percent of its iron, 55 percent of its gold, and 33 percent of its trade. If Shanghai remained China's commercial center, by 1931 Manchuria had become its industrial center." (Paine, 2012, 15).

Thus, it's not altogether surprising that Japan's invasion of Manchuria in 1931 resulted from a long, complex chain of historical events stretching back to the late 19th century. Approximately 380,000 square miles in extent, or 1.4 times the size of the American state of Texas, Manchuria came into Imperial Russia's possession in 1900 due to the "Boxer Rebellion" in China, but the Russians held it only briefly; their defeat in the Russo-Japanese War shook loose their control from important parts of Manchuria by the end of 1905.

The Japanese gained two important footholds in Manchuria thanks to their victory. One consisted of Port Arthur (renamed Ryojun by the Japanese), an economically and strategically vital harbor city on the Liaodung Peninsula, plus the peninsula itself. The other comprised the South Manchurian Railway, which the Russians gave to the Japanese as a prize of war, in lieu of a cash indemnity. The Japanese subsequently formed the South Manchurian Railway Company, mostly owned by the Japanese Army, and Japanese civilians began investing heavily in Manchuria's lucrative industries. Tens of thousands of entrepreneurs flooded into Manchuria, greatly strengthening Japan's interests in the area. The Japanese Army stepped up their presence in this economically vital region, creating a quasi-independent military force and government known as the "Kwantung Army."

Naturally, the Chinese also wanted their portion of the tempting Manchurian feast. Unable to go head to head with the organized, thoroughly militaristic Japanese, they sent some 6 million emigrant laborers and settlers into the area as a sort of "demographic occupation." Nominally Chinese but subject to massive Japanese investment and military infiltration, filled with bandits and rival chieftains, Manchuria hovered on the brink of another conflict in the 1920s.

The Kwantung Army deliberately shoved it over that brink in 1931, and the Japanese invasion and occupation of Manchuria is sometimes described as the true beginning of World War II. At the very least, it marked the expansion of Japan's imperial empire, its ongoing friction with China, and what would turn into a Chinese resistance campaign that would last nearly 15 years until the end of World War II. Given its importance, the invasion of Manchuria continues to be remembered as one of the seminal events of the 20th century.

The Japanese Invasion of Manchuria and the Rape of Nanking: The History of the Most Notorious Events of the Second Sino-Japanese War examines the important events in northeastern China. Along with pictures of important people, places, and events, you will learn about the invasion of Manchuria like never before.

The Rape of Nanking

"From a military point of view, the taking of Nanking may be considered a victory for the Japanese army but judging it from the moral law, it is a defeat and a national disgrace—which will hinder cooperation and friendship with China for years to come, and forever lose her the respect of those living in Nanking today." - Minnie Vautrin, missionary, writing in her diary during the Nanking Massacre (Hu, 2010, 41).

"When you're talking about the Japanese military, thievery and rape just come with the territory. We stabbed them with bayonets, cut open pregnant women and took out the child. I killed five or six of them myself. I used to do some pretty brutal things." - Kodaira Yoshio, former Japanese soldier (Honda, 2015, 122).

"This is the shortest day of the year, but it still contains twenty-four hours of this hell on earth." - Dr. Robert Wilson, diary entry in Nanking, December 21st, 1937 (Brook, 1999, 219).

Three days of plundering traditionally befell cities taken by storm, a fate usually avoided by those surrendering before the first attacking soldier penetrated beyond the outer walls. In Europe and areas influenced by Enlightenment thinkers, this practice faded rapidly after the Napoleonic Wars. In 1937, however, as the Imperial Army of Japan invaded China, this custom returned in a horrifying new form – the Rape of Nanking or the Nanking Massacre, a bloodbath lasting more than six weeks and possibly claiming more than a quarter of a million lives.

Even the Japanese participating in the Nanking Massacre provided no rationale for their actions. They made no effort to explain it as a measure to terrorize other Chinese cities into surrender, or even to extract the location of hidden valuables. Instead, the Rape appears on the page of history as a psychopathic orgy of sadism for sadism's sake. Insatiably driven by hatred and, apparently, an unabashed relish for cruelty, the Japanese soldiery abandoned any semblance of restraint.

Women of every age, from small children to ancient elders, suffered innumerable rapes, in many cases dying from the mass raping alone. Those who did not die from sexual assault suffered death in other forms – shot, decapitated, or tortured to death once the soldiers found themselves sexually exhausted. Other women suffered fatal sexual torture involving the introduction of sharp foreign objects into their vagina or the placement of firecrackers or live grenades inside. At least one soldier, Kodaira Yoshio, so enjoyed torturing women to death that he returned to Japan as a serial killer, treating his Japanese victims in the same fashion as Chinese women until caught and executed.

The Japanese hacked men to death, shot them, used them for live bayonet practice, drowned them, locked them in sheds and burned them, or buried them alive. Even farm animals suffered mutilation, shooting, or burning while locked in their barns. Unburied corpses lay in heaps everywhere, while the Japanese continued to harry and slaughter the survivors for week after week. A choking stench hung over the city in the summer heat.

A number of foreign people on the scene attempted to save some of the Chinese from the massacre and, in some cases, succeeded. Their neutral status gave them the ability to move around Nanking without – in most cases – suffering assault or murder by the swarms of Japanese troops glutting themselves endlessly on human pain and death. They also photographed the nearly inconceivable images of bloodshed, creating a stark, permanent record of one of World War II's leading atrocities.

Even Third Reich personnel in the city interceded in a sometimes futile effort to rescue victims from their tormentors. At the end of the city's long harrowing, the world knew clearly, if it did not before, that the Japanese of Tojo and Hirohito showed a very different spirit than the exquisitely genteel and chivalric men of the Russo-Japanese War of 1905. The fight against

Imperial Japan represented not merely an effort to avoid being conquered, but for survival itself.

The Japanese Invasion of Manchuria and the Rape of Nanking: The History of the Most Notorious Events of the Second Sino-Japanese War chronicles one of the most infamous events of the 20th century. Along with pictures of important people, places, and events, you will learn about the rape of Nanking like never before.

The Japanese Invasion of Manchuria and the Rape of Nanking: The History of the Most Notorious Events of the Second Sino-Japanese War

About Charles River Editors

Introduction

The Invasion of Manchuria

   Chapter 1: Manchuria Before the Invasion

   Chapter 2: The Mukden Incident

   Chapter 3: The Seizure of Manchuria

   Chapter 4: Japanese Manchuria and the Founding of Manchukuo

   Chapter 5: Settling Manchukuo

   Chapter 6: Fighting the Soviets

   Online Resources

   Bibliography

The Rape of Nanking

   Chapter 1: The Military Prelude to the Nanking Massacre

   Chapter 2: The Second Sino-Japanese War in 1937

   Chapter 3: The Battle of Nanking

   Chapter 4: The Start of the Nanking Massacre

   Chapter 5: Foreigners Prepare the Safety Zone

   Chapter 6: The Arrival of the Japanese

   Chapter 7: The Rape of Nanking

   Chapter 8: Postwar Justice and War Crimes Trials

   Online Resources

   Bibliography

The Invasion of Manchuria

Chapter 1: Manchuria Before the Invasion

Manchuria – and, indeed, China as a whole – swarmed with bandits, bandit chieftains, and warlords during the 1920s. Among them, Zhang Zuolin emerged as one of the most successful of these in Manchuria, and indeed enjoyed such success that he soon contemplated seizing the entirety of China. Zhang Zuolin initially worked with the Japanese, having persuaded them in 1903 to spare his life in exchange for his cooperation after they captured him.

By 1912, Zhang Zuolin had established himself as the warlord of Mukden, an important Manchurian city and later the scene of Japan's invasion of Manchuria. Though in many ways a typical warlord, Zhang worked to develop Manchurian industries, especially those under Chinese control. He balanced this with efforts to appease the Japanese, securing their temporary support as he extended his dominion over the entire region.

Zhang Zuolin

Initially, Manchuria prospered under the mustached, smooth-faced Zhang, and this prosperity, in turn, gave the former bandit and Chinese bannerman the money he needed to arm and equip ever larger military forces. Like a fungal infection, ambition spread throughout Zhang Zuolin's system, as he contemplated ever more grandiose projects. As his spending finally outstripped Manchuria's considerable resources, the warlord turned to the old method of opium sales to fund his projects.

As that was going on, from 1919-1922, the Japanese attempted to use the brutal Russian Civil War as an opportunity to seize North Manchuria and, in fact, take portions of Russian territory proper. The Americans and several other nations briefly entered the Russian Civil War, fighting against the Bolsheviks on behalf of the White Russians, but these nations soon withdrew, however, and the Japanese fought on alone.

As the 1920s passed, the civilian government of Japan and the Imperial Japanese Army (IJA) jockeyed for power. As time went on, the civilians got the worst of the struggle. The IJA occasionally managed to maneuver a military man into the premiership, at which times their power naturally expanded. Assassination of civilian premiers who opposed them grew into a more frequent and more effective tool of the Japanese military as the ambitious generals and admirals came to dominate Japan's future policy.

By 1931, the IJA represented an extremely powerful "state within a state." Unlike the situation in Nazi Germany or Soviet Russia, where the military elements completely took over the government, the Japanese Army never fully replaced the civilian administration. Instead, the military mushroomed into the dominant partner in a badly dysfunctional relationship, forcing the civilian administration to do the "heavy lifting" of keeping the nation functional, while co-opting the national resources for ever more grandiose empire-building projects on mainland Asia.

Civilian administrators who protested or obstructed the IJA's high-handed militaristic policy often met their fate from a bullet, knife, or samurai sword delivered by the hands of a convenient ultra-nationalist. Though the civilian government grew progressively more helpless to resist their violent Army puppet-masters, they still managed occasional, futile attempts at pushback against the IJA's dictates.

Manchuria represented a resource base in which the Army operated as the majority investor and owner. The South Manchurian Railway Company, in particular, proved both a "cash cow" for the IJA and a method of increasing the Army's influence in one of Japan's most important economic regions. All other business activity in the area depended heavily on the railroad, especially the many enterprises involved in export.

With such strong interests in Manchuria, the Japanese grew alarmed when Chiang Kai-Shek established his capital at the northern city of Nanking in 1928. Escalating tensions, the Japanese moved Army units into Shantung Province in that year, creating a blocking force capable of delaying any northward move by Chiang into Manchuria.

Chiang Kai-Shek

Even more threatening, perhaps, from the Army's perspective, the Chinese began building their own railroad lines into Manchuria in 1928 and 1929. The Kwantung Army's monopoly, secured via their ownership of the South Manchurian Railway Company, came under threat from these activities. Local Japanese businessmen, seeing their profits or even livelihood threatened by Chinese competition, pressured their government to take a hard line towards Manchuria.

A picture of Kwantung Army soldiers practicing maneuvers

With the selection of Tanaka Giichi as Prime Minister of Japan in 1927, Japan's Manchurian policy grew more expansionist – the aggressive phase of so-called "Tanaka Diplomacy." Zhang Zuolin advanced south into China proper, but he soon suffered reverses at the hands of the Nationalists commanded by Chiang Kai-Shek. Zhang retreated, and at this point, a split occurred in Japanese policy; Prime Minister Tanaka wished to keep Zhang as an ally and even work to strengthen his position, but the Kwantung Army independently decided to kill Zhang when he returned following his defeat by the Nationalists, believing his power and independent nature made him a threat to Japan's interests in Manchuria.

Tanaka Giichi

The instrument of assassination consisted of Colonel Komoto Daisaku, who proclaimed, "I will do it this time for sure…with the determination to settle everything of twenty years' standing once and for all" (Hata, 2008, 288). Komoto and several other Kwantung army officers rigged a bomb in a railway viaduct at the fringes of Mukden. On June 4th, 1928, the bomb exploded under Zhang Zuolin's personal train, inflicting wounds on the warlord which proved fatal within several hours.

The Kwantung Army believed that Zhang Xueliang, Zhang Zuolin's son, would prove easy to manipulate, which made sense because up until the moment of his father's death, Zhang Xueliang indulged himself in pleasure, engaging in an endless series of liaisons with various women and stupefying himself with opium. However, the assassination instilled in the "Young Marshal" rage and determination nobody had suspected of him until that moment. Zhang Xueliang, destined to die at age 100 at his house in Hawaii in 2001, loathed the Japanese and acted to shake off their yoke, offering his inherited holdings to the Nationalist government in

Nanking. Later, in 1936, Zhang Xueliang dramatically kidnapped Chiang Kai-Shek himself, forcing him to swear to ally with the Communists to expel the Japanese from China's soil. Chiang kept his word to an extent, though Mao Zedong paid only lip service to the anti-Japanese alliance, standing back to allow his enemies to immolate one another regardless of the cost to his nation.

Zhang Xueliang

Chapter 2: The Mukden Incident

The murder of Zhang Zuolin, intended to extend Kwantung Army control over Manchuria, instead accelerated the threat to Japan's influence in Manchuria. The Japanese Emperor wanted Colonel Komoto prosecuted for assassinating Zhang Zuolin, but Tanaka's government managed to change the charges to a mild reprimand for failing to guard the railroad diligently. Ultimately, the disgrace incurred by that ridiculously ironic judgment forced Tanaka's resignation in 1929, once again showing the complexity of Japan's prewar politics.

Despite that episode, the civilian government at home remained only partly aware of the

Kwantung Army's machinations, and all the while the organization cast about for a pretext to turn Manchuria into their fief.

Matters came to a head in 1931. In the Wanpaoshan Incident, Chinese farmers supported by Chinese police clashed with Korean farmers backed by Japanese police in Wanpaoshan, Manchuria. The Koreans won, but ensuing violence in Korea subsequently left more than 100 Chinese residents dead, and in In June of that year, Chinese troops killed IJA Captain Shintarō Nakamura and his companions in Manchuria, assuming them to be spies. The military tried to turn the Nakamuro Incident into an excuse for action, but by sensing the danger, the Chinese vigorously pursued Nakamuro's killers and deprived the Kwantung Army of yet another potentially promising opportunity to start a war.

Shintarō Nakamura and Entarō Isugi

Nevertheless, a general refusal by the Chinese to cooperate ultimately provided the Japanese with a solid pretext led to the Mukden Incident. Historians remain divided on real responsibility for the action. Some hold that the civilian government of Japan did not desire the outbreak of hostilities, and that the Kwantung Army acted independently, taking advantage of its distance from civilian authorities in the home islands to manufacture an incident against the Cabinet's and Emperor's wishes. Others acknowledge that the Kwantung Army took the initiative, but they believe the government dithered and looked the other way deliberately to give the military the opportunity to execute a plan whose benefits the Japanese government could reap if successful and deny should it fail. Yet others aver that Tokyo gave secret orders to the Kwantung officers who carried out the plan, moved by a largely unified desire to seize Manchuria among both civilian and Army authorities. Given the willingness of Japanese soldiers and officers to take responsibility and punishment (even execution) upon themselves to spare the Emperor even a hint of opprobrium, this latter theory remains possible.

Regardless of whatever machinations took place behind the scenes, two men, Lieutenant Colonel Ishiwara Kanji and Colonel Itagaki Seishiro, headed the actual plotters in Mukden. Ishiwara, a Nichiren Buddhist with a shaved head, and Itagaki, a mustached career officer hanged for war crimes after World War II, planned a false flag attack against the South Manchurian Railway for late September 1931. The timing coincided with the end of the harvest of sorghum or great millet, whose 10-foot stalks might otherwise interfere with rapid infantry marches across country.

Ishiwara

Itagaki

The Emperor and Army High Command dispatched Major General Tatekawa Yoshitsugu to Manchuria in September, ostensibly to bring the Kwantung Army back in check. Rather suspiciously, the outspoken opinions of Tatekawa ensured that everyone in the Japanese government already knew that he supported a military annexation of Manchuria, the exact event the government, army, and Emperor allegedly ordered him to prevent. Even more suspect, his commission called on him to meet specifically with the two leading Kwantung plotters, Ishiwara and Itagaki.

Yoshitsugu

When Tatekawa arrived on September 18th, 1931, Itagaki met him, accompanying him on the train into Mukden from a point several hours outside the city. Emperor Hirohito had once described Itagaki as the "stupidest man alive," but he possessed notable social skills and carried out his role to perfection. The two men's friends later recounted their conversation based on their own verbal accounts of it:

Itagaki: "You are well, sir, I hope."

Tatekawa: "Well, as a matter of fact, I have not slept much on the train and I hear you boisterous youngsters need discipline, but let's leave all that until we've had a good night's rest."

Itagaki: "We young men are also tired by our recent efforts, sir. So have no doubts about us but let me take you to a good inn when we arrive in Mukden and we will discuss business in the morning" (Bergamini, 1971, 442).

The "good inn" proved to be the Kikubumi, a Japanese geisha inn in Mukden. There, Tatekawa ate a superb dinner, drank quantities of alcohol, and, at 9:00 p.m. sharp, retired to his room with an attractive young geisha. In the meantime, a detachment of Japanese soldiers traversed the South Manchurian Railway line on handcars, disembarking at a point fairly close to the Peitaying Barracks, occupied by between 7,000 and 10,000 Chinese soldiers.

The Japanese soldiers placed dynamite charges near the rail line, setting them off to produce a thunderous explosion at 10:00 p.m. They then fired their rifles into the air in wild volleys to simulate a brief firefight. Though the Japanese later claimed the Chinese dynamited the tracks, destroying several yards, a scheduled passenger train coming south from Changchun hurtled through at 10:30 p.m. at top speed. Had a gap existed, derailment would have been unavoidable. However, the passengers later reported that they did not even feel a bump during the trip. The Japanese sappers had, in fact, deliberately detonated the dynamite a safe distance from the rails, inflicting no damage. Some of the plotters had suggested actually blowing up the train with a bomb, in the manner of Zhang Zuolin's assassination. More senior schemers disallowed this, not wishing to kill Japanese passengers – or be later charged with their murder if the truth emerged.

The tragic farce grew more transparent as it developed. Ishiwara's men deposited three freshly killed Chinese in uniform – possibly soldiers kidnapped earlier, or even a trio of luckless peasants dressed in military garb, then executed in cold blood – next to the undamaged railway tracks as "saboteurs shot while escaping." The Japanese pointed the heads of all three corpses towards the distant Peitaying Barracks in case anyone failed to understand the glaringly obvious scenario already constructed.

Two Russian 9.5 inch naval guns, brought into the town by the conspirators and based in a concrete battery built as a "swimming pool" earlier in the summer, opened fire on the Chinese barracks at 11:00 p.m. Not even bothering with the pretense of an investigation, the Japanese mustered their troops to attack the barracks, killing the guards, whose officers had equipped them only with dummy rifles due to their untrained state. Major General Tategawa slipped from the arms of his geisha and out the back door of the inn to join this force, though the geisha later swore he spent the entire night with her.

Meanwhile, Ishiwara reported to Lieutenant General Shigeru Honjō in Port Arthur, then taking a bath, to report on the situation. Though the Japanese initiated aggression against the Chinese, Ishiwara carefully cast his report to depict the opposite: "The odds against us are staggering. The entire countryside may rise. Offense is our only defense. I hope, sir, that you will allow Itagaki to proceed with the contingency plan that has already been prepared." (Bergamini, 1971, 445).

Honjō

Honjō made a great show of berating Itagaki over the telephone, but soon came to the actual point of the call: giving him permission to attack Mukden itself at 11:30 p.m.

The transparency of the Mukden Incident could hardly have increased; the Kwantung Army created a scenario in which an explosion in the darkness near a rail line at 10:00 p.m. could be ascribed so confidently to a secret Chinese plot that it justified an attack on the city just 90 minutes later – surely one of the most rapid forensic successes in history at a scene of random terrorism. Even Uchida Yasuya, the Japanese president of the South Manchurian Railway Company, deemed the situation a false flag attack: "The reason for military occupation is reportedly the destruction of the railway by Chinese troops from the North Barracks, but railway supervisors have been sent to the spot three times so far and have been refused entry […] The present military action has been practiced as an emergency exercise since the 14th […] and is assumed to be the execution of a prearranged plan." (Ogata, 1964, 63).

A picture of Japanese officials "inspecting" the railway

A picture of the supposedly sabotaged site

The Chinese soldiers evacuated their barracks – leaving 320 corpses behind, according to the Japanese – in accordance with their orders to avoid potentially war-triggering incidents even in the name of self-defense. The Japanese readily took both the barracks and the city of Mukden itself, at the cost of two men killed, possibly in accidents or by friendly fire. The troops shot 75 Chinese policemen in Mukden's streets.

Major General Hasebe Shogo attacked the city of Changchun the next day, leading part of the Japanese 2nd Division. The Chinese began a general retreat northward, towards the heavily Russia-influenced northern Manchuria and the city of Harbin, which provided the north's economic and political linchpin, similar to Mukden in the south. The Mukden Incident gave the Kwantung Army its desire, launching it on a trajectory of conquest.

A picture of Japanese troops entering Mukden during the Mukden Incident

Chapter 3: The Seizure of Manchuria

Bundesarchiv, Bild 102-12301
Foto: o.Ang. | September 1931

Picture of IJA infantry and artillery in Manchuria

Once hostilities began, various Japanese factions attempted to pursue different goals, but the situation inevitably developed towards the complete annexation of Manchuria. The Kwantung Army's wishes proved paramount due to the fact that its men and officers directly controlled events on the scene; so long as the government continued to supply it with reinforcements and money, the army could eventually circumvent any attempts at restraint that politicians in faraway Tokyo tried to initiate.

The Tokyo government made a show, at least, of trying to limit the damage. Initially, the Prime Minister responded to the news by ordering the Kwantung Army to limit its actions to Mukden itself, where the supposed "Incident" took place. However, the plotters had anticipated this and had arranged simultaneous seizure of many other towns in South Manchuria, so by the time the order arrived limiting action to Mukden, the army already controlled a number of other towns. Arguing that retreating from these other towns would result in chaos, making a war with China more, rather than less, likely, the Kwantung Army plotters successfully nullified the central government's objections.

With all the key locations of southern Manchuria in their hands, the military schemers turned to the matter of conquering the north. Lieutenant General Honjō Shigeru requested reinforcements from Japan, ostensibly to stabilize the situation through a largely defensive show of force. The government complied, authorizing the immediate dispatch of three more divisions to Manchuria.

Ishiwara, Itagaki, and the clique of officers they represented now wanted to move troops into Kirin, well within northern Manchurian territory. This represented a drastic expansion of Japanese occupation, causing even Honjō Shigeru to demur, but the plotters pushed as hard as they could to expand the operational area to Kirin. Japanese agents and "bomb-throwers" in Kirin stirred up chaos, while compliant Japanese residents peppered Honjō's headquarters with pleas for military protection against an alleged Chinese menace.

The Kwantung schemers concentrated the 2nd Division – the "Courageous Division" – at Changchun under the command of Lieutenant General Jirō Tamon on September 20th. The city's extensive railway facilities made it ideal as a jumping off point for an attack on Kirin, and due to the large numbers of troops eager to participate in the action, the Kwantung Army assembled a train of at least 60 cars, pulled by a trio of locomotives, to move them north.

Jirō

However, Honjō still refused to authorize a Kirin attack. Ishiwara attempted to persuade him, but after he was rebuffed, he left in a fury. Half a dozen top staff officers went to speak with Honjō in his hotel suite. One of them recorded the gist of the wrangling in his diary, referring to Honjō only as "the Commander" or "the Commander-in-Chief:" "Arai first explained the situation in Kirin, then Ishiwara urged a Kirin expedition from the standpoint of tactics and strategy, and Itagaki followed by expressing the need for resolutely pursuing the objective. An atmosphere of great strain prevailed. The Commander was greatly angered by Itagaki's statement, 'If the Kwantung Army wavers' […] He finally decided upon a Kirin expedition. The time was 3:00 A.M. [...] The Commander-in-Chief was in great distress." (Ogata, 1964, 64).

In the end, the conspirators won Honjō's assent without playing their trump card: the threat of mass resignation. Itagaki conveyed the news to the waiting officers of the 2nd "Courageous" Division, who greeted it with a roar of "Banzai!" With that, packed troop-train thundered north from Changchun on the 21st to take Kirin.

At this point, the fiery commander of Japanese forces in occupied Korea, General Senjūrō Hayashi, took a fateful hand in affairs. General Hayashi sent multiple telegraphs to Tokyo, starting on the 19th, requesting permission to send troops from Korea to Manchuria to support the Kwantung Army. On the 21st, learning of the Kirin expedition, Hayashi sent 4,000 men and two squadrons of aircraft across the border into Manchuria without imperial permission.

Hayashi took an immense risk in doing so, as an order to commit *seppuku* might have resulted. However, Emperor Hirohito, though expressing personal disgust, eventually endorsed the maneuver. Hayashi's reckless gamble contributed greatly to the total conquest of Manchuria, while earning him the sobriquet of "The Border-Jumping General."

Senjūrō Hayashi

Chaotic fighting and additional territorial seizures continued into October. The Kwantung Army suffered a temporary disappointment when the government forbade Harbin's seizure despite the best efforts of Japanese agitators in the city to spark an "incident." However, in mid-October, the Chinese burned three north Manchurian railroad bridges on the line leading to Tsitsihar in an effort to limit the 2nd "Courageous" Army's mobility. Delighted, the ailing but clever Ishiwara pointed out that the Kwantung Army must protect Japanese economic interests, whatever the government feared; Manchuria enjoyed a bumper soybean harvest that year, and the Japanese South Manchurian Railway provided the means for exporting the vast quantities of beans and oil to the ports, and thence globally. Japan's economy needed the boost provided by sales of Manchurian soybeans to Europe, America, and every other corner of the planet.

The convenient and thoroughly exploited "mission creep" continued. The Tokyo government authorized the Kwantung Army to protect the repair parties sent out to rebuild the three bridges over the Nonni River, and the local military commanders naturally interpreted this in the broadest manner possible.

At this moment, the Japanese encountered the one element with a remaining chance at spoiling their plans – a relatively competent opponent. One of the most interesting figures of the Japanese invasion of Manchuria emerged into the spotlight in the person of General Ma Chan-shan (also known as Ma Zhanshan), a Chinese Muslim warlord with a steady gaze and a long, slender mustache, resembling a figure from the time of the Golden Horde.

Ma Chan-shan

As Colonel Hamamoto Kisaburo's 800 infantry arrived at the Nonni River, Ma Chan-shan's artillery brought them under heavy fire. The Chinese and Manchurians initially repulsed Hamamoto's counterattack. Hamamoto contemplated a suicidal banzai charge, but Ishiwara arrived and, quick-witted as ever despite being in considerable pain from a kidney ailment, talked the colonel into awaiting reinforcements. The reinforcements duly arrived, including an infantry battalion and aircraft, and the Japanese forced Ma's men to retreat on November 6th. The Chinese suffered 200 KIA, while inflicting 36 deaths and wounding 144 Kwantung soldiers in return. Ma Chan-shan retreated in good order, however, with an enhanced reputation as a Chinese patriot.

The Japanese and Ma Chan-shan soon clashed again. With the bridges repaired, the Kwantung Army failed to retreat again but instead mustered their forces and then advanced on Tsitsihar. The attack involved a reinforced infantry division (the 2nd, plus troops from Korea) with air support. Occurring in bitterly cold weather around -20 Fahrenheit, with strong winds blowing out of the north, the attack met fierce resistance by Ma's Chinese. *The Sydney Morning Herald* reported on the action in its Thursday, November 19th edition, describing Ma's counterattack against the invading force as an attack, possibly due to Japanese sources: "A severe battle was fought to-day at Tashing, a small town near Tsitsihar. General Ma Chan-shan, the Chinese general, launched an offensive on the Japanese positions. The engagement is described as the most severe for the past few days. The troops are suffering great hardships owing to the severe cold. Chinese throughout the country are rallying to General Ma Chan-shan's support." (Sydney Herald, 1931, 9).

Though the Japanese once again forced a Chinese retreat, they paid bitterly for their success. The IJA's own records, kept secret until after the war, revealed that the Chinese killed around 400 Japanese and wounded 278, losing 300-600 dead and several thousand wounded in return. The Japanese also sustained 996 frostbite casualties, or nearly 17% of their 5,900 men.

Recognizing the menace of Ma Chan-shan, the Japanese took an extraordinary measure. On December 7th and 8th, Itagaki and four other officers secretly visited the General's headquarters to sway him to the Kwantung Army side. One of the four officers was the infamous Doihara Kenji, nicknamed "Lawrence of Manchuria." Colonel Doihara, a master of every kind of underhanded activity, later recruited criminal gangs to strengthen Japanese control and managed Japan's opium trade in Manchuria. Knowing mere words would never sway Ma Chan-shan, the Japanese offered the illiterate warlord $3 million in gold. Ma Chan-shan accepted the cash gladly, apparently heartily endorsing the Japanese as the new masters of Manchuria. He did not disband his troops, instead ostensibly adding them to the allied contingents of warlords who had chosen to throw in their lot with the Kwantung Army.

Kenji

The Japanese secured the final major north Manchurian objective of Harbin, with its 100,000 anti-communist Russian expatriates and numerous Chinese commercial interests, in early February 1932. Ironically, the impetus for the takeover came from an appeal issued by Chinese merchants themselves. The armies of two Chinese warlords clashed near the city in January, leading to the businessmen appealing to the only force of greater power available, the Kwantung Army. Eager to seize the opportunity offered by this invitation, the Japanese paid cash up front to the Chinese Eastern Railway for the railroad fares of every soldier they sent to Harbin in order to ensure the strongest regional company raised no objections to their presence. Once again, the 2nd "Courageous" Division provided the bulk of the forces used, and the Japanese took Harbin at the loss of only a few dozen men.

With Harbin in their hands, the Kwantung Army estimated they possessed the means necessary to unite north and south Manchuria into a new state. This puppet nation, Manchukuo, or "Manchu Land," would exist under the nominal rulership of Henry Puyi, the last Qing Emperor, ousted from the throne in 1912 and restored briefly in 1917 by a warlord fighting against the struggling Republic of China. Puyi, getting wind of the Kwantung Army's ambitions in Manchuria, thought he might use the Japanese to restore him to his imperial throne.

Accordingly, in late 1931, he wrote to the Japanese. Soon, Doihara and Itagaki contacted him and proposed he head the soon to be constituted state of Manchukuo. Puyi responded favorably, moving to Port Arthur to be close to the action. The Japanese left him kicking his heels for some time, which infuriated the touchy monarch, thoroughly conscious of his own "divine" dignity and impatient to regain the pomp and power he had lost. Then, on February 23rd, 1932, Itagaki met him in person, suggesting that he become the Chief Executive of the new state of Manchukuo. This plan brought Puyi's fury to the boiling point, as he described in his autobiography: "The phrase 'Your Excellency' enraged me. My blood rushed to my face. Never before had I been thus addressed by the Japanese, and I was not prepared to tolerate the abolition of my imperial title [...] I was so worked up I could scarcely sit still. 'If names are not right then speech will not be in order,' I shouted, 'and if speech is not in order then nothing will be accomplished!'" (Puyi, 2010, 136).

Nevertheless, Itagaki managed to smooth over the situation, apologizing profusely and making many polite, smiling statements, while concealing his own emotions as deftly as novelist John P. Marquand's fictional Kwantung Army agent Mr. Moto. Itagaki promised that the title of Chief Executive would only exist temporarily, with the Manchukuo constitution soon restoring the title of Qing Emperor. In closing his remarks, he also informed Puyi almost in passing that refusal would be taken as the sign of a hostile attitude. Puyi confessed in his memoirs that this statement, while in the depths of Kwantung Army territory, terrified him. Puyi assented, though he and his advisers found themselves full of doubts and foreboding about the future.

Puyi

On February 28th, 1932, the Japanese convened the All-Manchurian Assembly of Mukden, including General Ma Chan-shen, to decide on the future of Manchuria. The assembly, a rubber stamp for Kwantung Army plans, proposed the formation of Manchukuo with Henry Puyi as the Chief Executive. In a piece of dramatic farce worked out in advance, the Assembly sent nine representatives to Puyi in Port Arthur on March 1st, asking him to act as Chief Executive of the new state. As prearranged with the Japanese, Puyi loftily declined. On March 5th, 29 delegates arrived and pleaded with Puyi in extravagant terms to accept the weighty responsibility. After a proper show of imperial coyness, "Henry" accepted their proposal, and traveled to the new capital of Manchukuo at Changchun with his wife and household.

Puyi expected to wield at least some power, but the Japanese almost immediately underlined his status as a glamorously-costumed figurehead whom the Kwantung Army could unmake and kill in a moment if it wished. As Puyi wrote, "I soon discovered that the power and authority of the Chief Executive were only shadows without substance." (Puyi, 2010, 142). The Japanese did not even allow him to leave his mansion in Changchun for a stroll without advance permission and an escort of Japanese police and soldiers. These men allegedly protected Puyi and his family, but in reality they prevented their escape.

The throne for Puyi in occupied Manchuria

Puyi as the "emperor"

Chapter 4: Japanese Manchuria and the Founding of Manchukuo

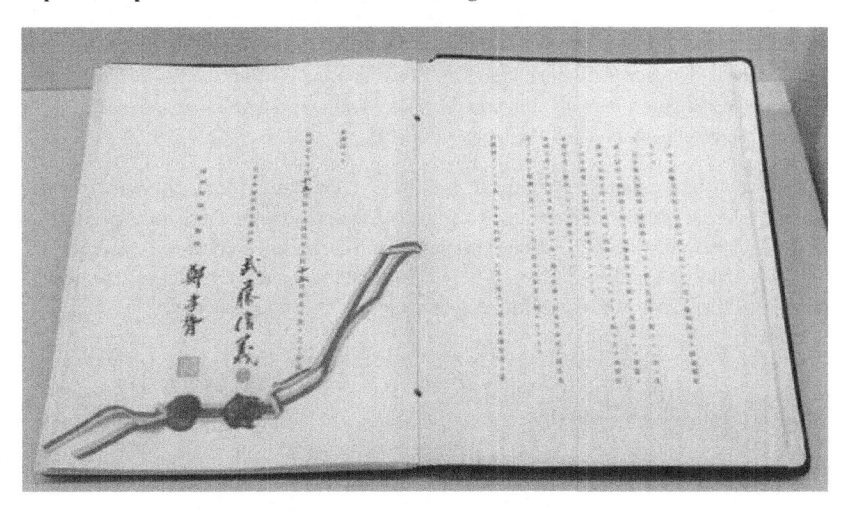

The Japan-Manchukuo Protocol (September 15, 1932)

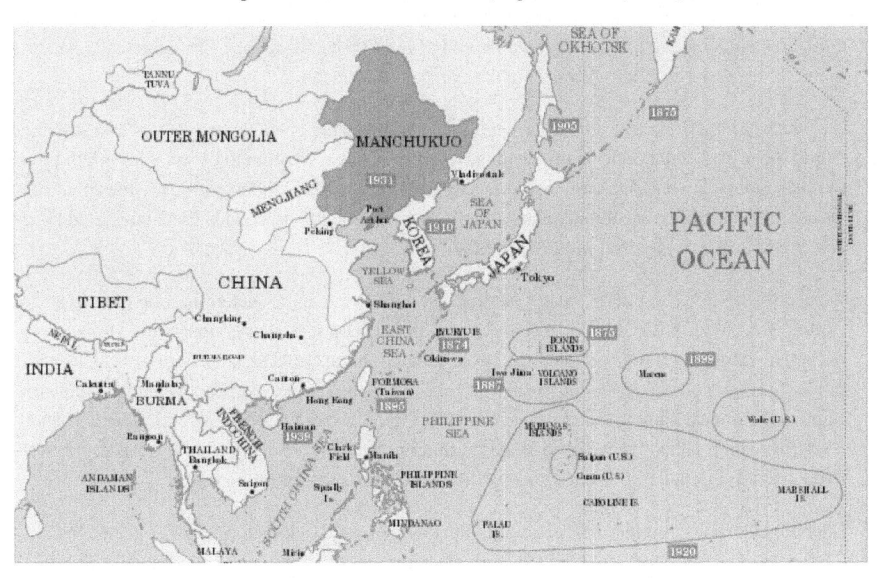

A map with the puppet state of Manchukuo

Using the resources at their disposal, brazen lies, false flag attacks, and the supine attitude of the home government (if not its secret collusion), the Kwantung Army conquered Manchuria, established the state of Manchukuo, created a puppet government under direct Army control, and set the stage for further strikes against China and possibly the Soviet Union. With its own resource and power base, the Imperial Japanese Army grew even more unmanageable by the civilian government than had already been the case.

Manchukuo remained troublesome, however, as it was still filled with conflict, hostile warlords, Chinese patriots, and bandits. The most startling reverse for the Japanese came from Ma Chan-shen, who secretly maintained his hatred of the invaders even when he accepted their gold. In fact, the cunning general, completely outwitting even practiced, ruthless schemers like Ishiwara and Doihara, worked as a fifth columnist inside Kwantung territory.

Using the gold given to him as a bribe to switch sides, augmented by as much additional funding as he could prize from the Japanese, Ma Chan-shen recruited a horde of both infantry and cavalry, equipping them at IJA expense. Leaving on an "inspection tour" in April, he soon revealed his resolve to continue fighting Japan, mustering an army of around 300,000 men with the power of his name and his reputation for patriotism.

Ma Chan-shen's forces continued to be a thorn in the Japanese side for the rest of the occupation. The General eventually joined the Nationalist Chinese forces during the prolonged and bitter Sino-Japanese Wars, and, at the end of his life, he chose the Communist side. He died in 1950, respected as a hero of his country even by Mao Zedong.

Undeterred, the Japanese continued vigorous actions against bandits both actual and so-called, filling the towns under their control with severed heads as a warning to others who might think to rebel against Kwantung Army authority. The history of Manchukuo remained one of constant "brushfire" conflict, occasionally exploding into outright battle as the Japanese struggled to control their newly acquired Imperial possession.

Despite the strife, and perhaps as a natural response to it, Japan's determination to hold and exploit Manchukuo hardened, especially as the global economic depression of the 1930s deepened. Arguably, the Great Depression originated in the "gold standard" system, whose fatally limited money supply could not keep pace with the rapid expansion of modern industrial economies, thus leading to a crash by choking off the means of conducting commerce. Those countries which jettisoned the gold standard quickly recovered swiftly from the crisis; those slow to abandon the tempting but disastrous yellow metal suffered for many years.

Japan suffered economic contraction, lending a keen edge to its imperialistic hunger, but China, on the other hand, used the silver standard, providing a much more expansive, flexible money supply. The country enjoyed a competitive advantage during the 1930s despite civil war, with an expanding economy that benefited from the golden shackles holding back other major economies. The industrial might thus created continues to make China a major manufacturing power in the early 21st century.

Throughout the decade, the Japanese worked hard to develop the economies of Korea, Taiwan, and Manchuria to make up for the resource deficiencies of their island nation. Japan invested approximately 9 billion yen in Manchukuo, combining this with a thoroughgoing modernization program. Despite the brutality of the Kwantung Army, the swarms of bandits and anti-Japanese partisans, and the essentially exploitative aims of the occupiers, Manchuria enjoyed explosive economic growth under the Japanese. The expansion program followed a roughly rational trajectory. First, the Japanese built enormous additions to the railroad and road systems, doubling the amount of railway track and creating the first modern roads in many areas. This infrastructure construction laid the groundwork for the following industrial "miracle."

As the level of activity in Manchuria increased, the Kwantung Army and Japanese business groups entered a partly hostile and partly cooperative relationship in developing Manchuria. Many high army officials wanted to exclude both financial (banking) influence and that of politics in general. However, the IJA also managed to project an almost welcoming image at times, as shown by the statement of a Japan Chamber of Commerce member in March 1932, shortly after the installation of Henry Puyi as the Chief Executive of Manchukuo: "We talked with all the key military authorities there as well as important people in and out of government. The military authorities really welcome the investment of domestic capital, and I did not see evidence of the army oppressing capitalists. We at home will take the opportunity to give as much financial support as possible to the construction of the new Manchuria." (Young, 1998, 196).

While the Japanese benefited from the arrangement, the inhabitants of Manchukuo did so at a much lower level, or not at all. The per capita income in Manchuria rose by a startling 50% under the Japanese, but Manchuria produced no consumer goods. All economic activity focused on creating goods to export (providing Japan with money) or extracting raw materials for Japanese industry.

With no domestic products to buy with their new, higher wages, Manchukuo's workers turned to the only source of consumer goods available – Japan. The colony provided a literally captive market to which Japanese business exported its surplus products. This helped to lift Japan out of its depression by 1933, along with abandonment of the stifling gold standard. In effect, the Japanese paid the Manchurian people to extract materials and send them to Japan; Japan's businesses turned those materials into goods; and the Manchurian workers then used their wages to buy those products.

The Japanese Industrial Club's official statement summed up the plan and the relationship neatly: "As much as possible Manchuria should be made into a supplier of materials. It is a mistake to encourage new industrial production that will compete with Japanese domestic industry [...] Manchurian tariffs should be kept as low as possible to encourage the import of Japanese products. Industrial goods should be produced within Japan and exported to Manchuria." (Young, 1998, 204).

In political terms, the Japanese created a hybrid administration based on both Chinese models and the government of Japan. However, the Kwantung Army was the only stakeholder represented. They behaved in a high-handed manner repugnant to the populace, though enforcing law and order of a sort.

Somewhat echoing the tyrannical laws of the former Tokugawa Shogunate in Japan, the Japanese moved the population of Manchuria into new cities and fortified villages, rendering them far easier to control. The walls of the villages, allegedly built to guard against bandits, served as a type of prison system also. The Japanese progressively restricted movement in an effort to control the ordinary people.

While the Japanese built many schools, they meted out appalling treatment to Manchurian children, even as Japanese children received favors and good treatment. Although the Japanese settlers never rose above 2% of the population, they soon owned 25% of Manchukuo's superbly fertile arable land. The Manchukuo government preferred repression and violence to any effort to win the people over to their side, thus ensuring their artificial state remained artificial and always ready to implode.

Like many warlords before them, including the assassinated Zhang Zuolin, the Japanese turned to opium and alcohol to provide revenue streams from their new acquisition. Alcohol production centered on beer, an originally Russian industry from Harbin, and by 1938, Japanese breweries produced 800,000 cases of beer annually. Japanese businessmen also moved into the age-old wine production characteristic of China.

The opium trade formed a much more notorious part of the Japanese business plan. Doihara entered into the "black smoke" business avidly, generating a significant revenue stream for Manchukuo. Though missionaries and Chinese opponents of the Japanese alike exaggerated the effects of opium considerably, it still had an unfortunate effect on its victims. Approximately 250 opium shops existed in Harbin, a city of around 550,000 people, or 1 per 2,200 individuals.

A number of records exist of Chinese selling their wives in order to finance their opium habit. The emaciated corpses of dead addicts found their final resting place on the "ash heap of Harbin" outside one of the city gates, where they formed meals for scavengers or simply became entombed in garbage. The Japanese military expressed their attitude towards opium and their racism simultaneously in a savage pamphlet of the era: "The use of narcotics is unworthy of a superior race like the Japanese. Only inferior races, races that are decadent like the Chinese, the Europeans, and the East Indians, are addicted to the use of narcotics. This is why they are destined to become our servants and eventually disappear." (Smith, 2012, 42).

While the Japanese definitely participated in the opium trade, the Chinese pursued it just as vigorously, as did Korean emigres – facts conveniently forgotten in pro-China rhetoric used during Japanese occupation and following Japan's defeat. The Japanese did, however, utter many high-flown phrases about freeing addicts from the scourge of opium by instituting a limiting monopoly, while actually seizing as much profit as possible.

Chapter 5: Settling Manchukuo

Once they secured Manchuria and formed the puppet state of Manchukuo, the Japanese government sought to extend their permanent control over the region by moving numerous settlers there. Recruiters moved through Japan, enthusiastically seeking out volunteers to move to the new Imperial territory. The government had planned to move 5 million people to Manchukuo over the course of the next two decades, and they had succeeded in settling 270,000 before the end of World War II.

Though technically voluntary, refusal to go required delicate handling, since moving to Manchukuo as a "farmer-settler" possessed an aura of sublime patriotism, and in the ultra-nationalist, Army-controlled Japan of the 1930s, perceived lack of patriotism could cause harassment and even danger.

Moreover, many of those recruited – students, university professors, and the like – represented poor choices for the rigors of colonial farming life. The IJA had a special mission in mind for these unfortunate settlers, also. Most of the settlements stood on land close to the border between Manchukuo and the Soviet Union, so the male head of each household would also occupy the unenviable role of a militia soldier impeding the advance of the Red Army juggernaut in the event of a Russian attack.

Sato Tadao, a film historian, managed to elude recruitment as a settler without detrimental effects to himself. He described the situation into which the IJA placed the settlers sent to Manchuria: "Of course. the settlers were going to do more than just cultivate the land, since they would also serve as sort of farmer-soldiers, prepared to do battle against the Soviets if necessary. They were made aware of the danger of bandit attacks but were assured that they would have the protection of the Kwantung Army, which even within the indomitable Japanese army was considered an elite force." (Birnbaum, 2015, 134).

When the time came near the end of World War II, the men mostly fulfilled their duties, dying vainly in 1945 when the Soviets rushed across the border, while many of their families died at their own hands or those of the Kwantung soldiers ostensibly protecting them. Incredibly, the Japanese government was so determined to hide the news of imminent defeat in 1945 that it would continue sending thousands of settlers to Manchuria up to the moment when the Soviet T-34/85 tanks rolled across the border. Many of these people arrived just in time to flee, suffer rape and murder, or die of thirst, hunger, and exposure on the roads.

Before all that, however, the settlers mostly initially enjoyed their new homeland, unaware of the ghastly death awaiting them in the near future. Many came from cities or tiny subsistence farms, but in Manchuria, they established large family farms on the extremely rich, fertile alluvial soil near the rivers. For a few years, these people believed they had found "paradise."

The fiercer spirits found employment as "China ronin," named for the ronin, or masterless samurai, who participated as mercenaries in the wars of feudal Japan. Assisting local warlords or hunting bandits, these individuals helped to maintain Japan's grasp over the still-turbulent land of Manchukuo.

Despite the settlers, Manchukuo remained overwhelming Chinese in ethnic terms. The IJA conducted a census in 1940, whose results indicated the Japanese as the smallest minority at 2 percent, behind even the Mongols, whose population stood at 3 percent (Paine, 2012, 25). The Manchus proper, whom the Japanese speciously claimed as belonging to the same race as themselves, comprised 6 percent of Manchukuo's population. The vast bulk of the people, 85 percent, belonged to the Han Chinese ethnicity.

Chapter 6: Fighting the Soviets

The Japanese built a relatively successful economy in Manchukuo (at least from their own point of view), but the new state represented a foreign policy disaster from the first. The League of Nations famously condemned the invasion on February 28th, 1932, and Yōsuke Matsuoka walked out of the League on March 27th, with Japan thus embracing its status as a rogue state to the full. Before he did, however, Matsuoka made a bizarre, ranting speech which could scarcely have endeared him or his nation to many of the League members either: "Humanity crucified Jesus of Nazareth two thousand years ago [...] Japan stands ready to be crucified! But we do believe, and firmly believe, that, in a very few years, world opinion will be changed and that we also shall be understood by the world as Jesus of Nazareth was." (Paine, 2012, 35).

Matsuoka

    The Japanese originally intended to use Manchuria as a springboard to further conquests in Soviet territory as part of a long-term "Go-North" strategy. In fact, once Hitler's armies launched the Barbarossa offensive against Russia in 1941, the Japanese originally intended to attack as well, using the Kwantung Army as the core for an offensive into Russia. However, chaotic planning at the last minute led to the Japanese abandoning this relatively solid plan in favor of striking southeast and directing aggression against the United States. Many officers and generals deplored this choice, and even the war journal of a man at Imperial General

Headquarters noted, "Since even Hitler could err, it is understandable for our 2nd [Intelligence] Bureau to have made a mistake, too. The German forces' combat will drag out until the end of the year. I am deeply moved when I think of the changes in content that have taken place in our national policy since June. What lies in store for our empire? Dark clouds are hanging low; it is truly impossible to predict matters." (Coox, 1985, 1050).

Though second-guessing historical alternatives is impossible, an Axis victory over the Soviet Union would have been far more likely had the Japanese attacked the USSR from the east while Hitler struck it from the west. It is axiomatic that in war, concentration of force is key to victory. Instead of concentrating forces against the most formidable Old World opponent of the Axis, Russia, the Japanese military instead chose to diffuse the Axis' strength by opening a new front in a direction that led to conflict against the Americans, which proved a costly error.

The Japanese clearly overlooked some opportunities potentially provided by their imperial territory by paying no attention whatsoever to local goodwill, but they showed prescience in one important area. Attempting to gain international support for their new puppet regime by portraying it as a barrier zone preventing the spread of Marxist doctrines from the Soviet Union to the teeming millions of China, the Japanese government warned accurately, "Communism has already invaded China, and the alarming extent and success of the invasion is far too seldom realized. A communized China would constitute a problem for Europe and America beside which other questions would pale into insignificance (Paine, 2012, 122).

Mao would more than prove this concern justifiable, but Japan's startling brutality – particularly during the war in north China (which included the Rape of Nanking) – and its clashes with Western interests ensured that the West disregarded these arguments. Anti-communist foreign countries also tended to rely on Chiang Kai-Shek's Nationalist Kuomintang movement to control the Marxists in China. Ultimately, no matter how steadfast Japan actually was against communism, the Japanese fomented chaos and disunity in China, eventually helping Mao emerge victorious after World War II.

The conquest of Manchuria represented a watershed in Japan's 20th century history. From that moment onward, the Army controlled the destiny of the nation, running amok in pursuit of open-ended territorial seizure ended only by the reluctant but powerful intervention of the United States in World War II. Thus, it should come as no surprise that the Japanese Army never considered limiting its ambitions to Manchuria. In fact, expansionism continued without pause, even before Manchukuo lay fully under Japanese control.

The Manchurian success gave the Army a dominant position relative to the civilian government for a variety of reasons, ranging from the popularity achieved thanks to Manchurian economic spoils to the creation of an independent financial base. However, the shadow of the Soviet Union continued to hang over Manchukuo for the whole of its 14-year existence, and trouble erupted at the border between Mongolia – then the Mongolian People's Republic – and

Manchukuo in 1939. Since the area bore the name Nomonhan, the struggle acquired the sobriquet of the Nomonhan Incident. As usual, both sides called it an "Incident" to avoid the need to declare war.

The two sides drew the border at a different point in the empty landscape, with its sand dunes and thickets of stunted willows. The Japanese averred the border lay at the Khalkhyn Gol river, while the Mongols claimed the border lay 12 miles east of the watercourse. Since no official agreement ever fixed the border, the question is moot. The territory would probably best be described as "disputed" – the precise type of undefined no-man's land that engenders violent international incidents between semi-hostile powers.

The first skirmishes occurred on May 5th and May 11th-12th, 1939, with bands of a few dozen Mongol horsemen clashing with truck-borne Manchu troops – mostly Manchurian Mongols in Japanese service, known as Barguts – and Japanese border police. The Japanese claimed that the Mongols attempted to build positions in Japanese territory, while the Mongols asserted the Japanese attacked them unprovoked while they patrolled or grazed their horses on the Khalkhyn Gol's east bank.

Mongolian cavalry during the fighting

The Soviets took alarm at these clashes, not wholly without justification. At the time of the Mukden Incident, the USSR attempted to create a nonaggression pact with the Japanese, but the latter eschewed the treaty, signaling the strong possibility of future hostile intent. Of course, the Soviets also had territorial ambitions; besides their abortive attack on Poland in the 1920s – expressly made in an effort to penetrate into and conquer a Germany weakened by World War I – they signed the Molotov-Ribbentrop Pact in 1939, effectively carving up Eastern Europe between the Third Reich and Soviet empires.

As the border incidents continued, the Kwantung Army issued a directive seemingly calculated to ensure the maximum level of escalation: "[T]he frequency and escalation of incidents can only be prevented by the resolute application of just punishment, the basic principle being neither to invade nor to permit invasion […] in areas where the lines of demarcation are unclear, the officer responsible for defending the border shall himself determine the demarcation line." (Sella, 1983, 672-673). These orders, of course, effectively translated to "there is no fixed border, attack if you wish."

With skirmishes continuing, the Soviets sent Marshal Georgiy Zhukov to the Khalkhyn Gol area on June 1st. Both on May 28th and June 22nd, major aerial dogfights occurred between Soviet and Japanese fighter aircraft. At this point, both sides used relatively primitive airplanes with oxygen problems, limiting their service ceiling and exposing them to constant ground fire.

A destroyed Soviet airplane

The respective railway systems of the two empires gave Japan a theoretical logistics advantage, with major rail heads lying just 120 miles from the Khalkhyn Gol battlefield. Russian supplies, meanwhile, arrived by train more than 400 miles from the battlefield, with subsequent transport relying on trucks traversing low-quality Mongolian roads. In practice, however, the Japanese system broke down due to a serious deficiency in trucks, while Zhukov deployed 2,600 vehicles to keep his soldiers constantly supplied.

Picture of Soviet troops and a tank during the fighting

The Japanese attacked across the Khalkhyn Gol in July, but after fierce fighting in which they suffered 5,000 casualties while inflicting even more on the Soviets, their offensive ground to a halt. Lack of supplies and artillery forced the Kwantung soldiers to cease offensive operations and hold their positions.

In August 1939, Zhukov struck back with three rifle divisions, a pair of reinforced tank divisions numbering some 600 tanks, 550 aircraft, and two divisions of Mongolian cavalry. The Russians sustained and inflicted heavy losses, but they still crushed the Japanese decisively. By this time, many Japanese soldiers suffered so heavily from starvation they could no longer fight or retreat, simply collapsing on the field as the effort of combat used up their last reserves of strength. Many proved too weak even to successfully commit suicide. The Soviets took many prisoners, but these men were considered traitors by their own side and could not return even when released. Some lived in tents years later around the fringes of Manchukuo's civilization, describing themselves as the dead.

A picture of captured Japanese prisoners

Following the Battles of Khalkhyn Gol, the Soviets and Japanese remained warily aloof from one another's spheres of influence until August 1945. By then, the Americans had finished campaigns in Iwo Jima and Okinawa, and the writing was on the wall for Japan, no matter how zealously their soldiers and civilians held out. The Soviets hoped to take a piece of the pie before Japan formally capitulated.

Despite earlier American urging to enter the Pacific Theater, the Soviets had refused to declare war on Japan prior to the Third Reich's defeat in May 1945. Stalin, regardless of his startlingly poor grasp of tactics and primitive fixation on offensive actions even when utterly inappropriate, clearly grasped the fact that a two-front war might spell the end of the Soviet Union. Meanwhile, the Japanese had their hands full with the Americans, and they remained mostly content to observe a sort of undeclared armistice with Russia.

In turn, Hitler's hopes for a decisive Japanese role foundered on the rock of Japanese pragmatism. The Empire of the Rising Sun pursued its own interests, fighting a largely separate war and hastening the United States' entry into the conflict, all to the Germans' detriment. Heinz Guderian, one of Nazi Germany's most successful generals, noted and agreed with a general consensus among the Wehrmacht soldiery that the Japanese alliance represented a lethal error: "The soldiers wondered at the time why, when Hitler declared war on America, Japan did not do likewise against the Soviet Union. A direct consequence of this was that the Russian forces in the Far East remained available for use against the Germans. [...] The result of this policy of Hitler's was not an alleviation of our difficulties, but an additional burden of almost incalculable weight." (Guderian, 1964, 138).

Once Hitler was dead and Germany fell, the Soviet Union moved without hesitation against Japan. This apparently caught Tokyo completely at unawares, in part due to the fact that the American offensive had finished off Okinawa and President Harry S. Truman, anticipating massive American casualties, ordered atomic bombs deployed against Japan. The nuclear bombings would occur, purely by chance, at the same time as the Soviet offensive.

Forged by the failures and successes of World War II into a dangerous, professional force quite different from the pitifully untrained and barely-equipped hordes butchered by the million during Nazi Germany's invasion of Russia a few years earlier, the Red Army delivered a stunning knockout punch to Japan's occupation of Manchuria in August 1945. Deploying a million men in a crushing surprise attack, Stalinist Russia conquered Manchuria in a two-week campaign reminiscent of an early-war Wehrmacht blitzkrieg.

The Soviet scheme for seizing Manchuria involved a grand scale strategic envelopment demanding consummate professionalism from the Red Army's commanders and aggression, initiative, and tactical prowess on the part of the lower echelons. The brilliant, forceful success achieved underlined just how thoroughly the war years honed the Soviet army into a lethal fighting machine, rather than a mass of unfortunate rabble.

The plan, known to the Soviets as the Manchurian Strategic Offensive Operation, involved three separate "fronts" comprised of 11 armies. Each army operated both as part of the overall plan and with considerable independent flexibility. The somnolent Kwantung Army crumpled before this attack as is before a steel landslide.

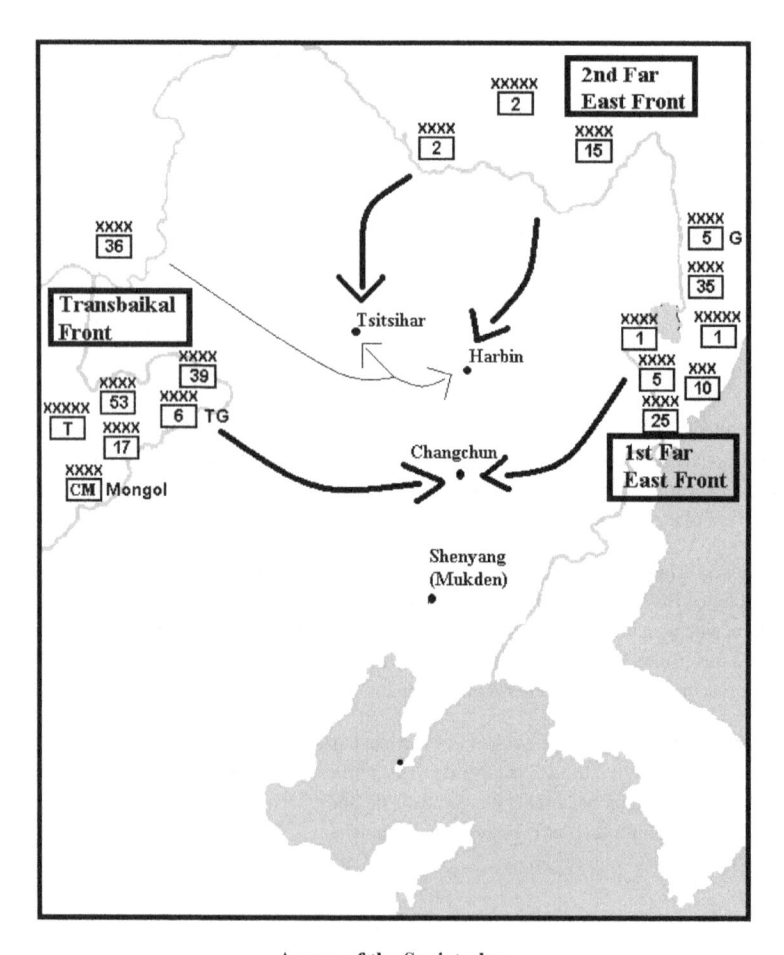

A map of the Soviet plan

Overall leadership of the Far East Command lay with Marshal Aleksandr M. Vasilevsky, an experienced campaigner twice named a Hero of the Soviet Union. A fleshy-faced man who would have preferred a career as an agronomist, Vasilevsky began preparing the Manchurian Operation's complex, many-layered plans in late 1944. In June 1945, he traveled to eastern Russia and began an exhaustive series of rehearsals with the commanders and troops put at his disposal.

Vasilevsky in 1945

At the eastern edge of Manchukuo's border, the Japanese had erected a powerful line of fortifications across all the easily passable terrain, resting the flanks of this formidable obstacle on forested mountains. The Soviets, however, had studied the Wehrmacht and consciously emulated its successes. Marshal Kirill Meretskov, commanding the 1st Far Eastern Front, aimed to duplicate the German success in bypassing the Maginot Line through the Ardennes Forest at the war's beginning.

General Shiina Masataka faced Meretskov's sledgehammer with the 124th Infantry Division of the Japanese Army, defending approximately 25 miles of fortifications alongside other units, particularly the 126th and 128th Infantry Divisions. At the time of the Soviet attack, these men were still building additional fortifications, indicating how little the Kwantung Army expected an attack. Conversely, the Soviets constructed an immense network of vertical camouflage walls and overhead covers on the roads, enabling them to move their assault troops forward without the Japanese realizing. Meretskov massed the Soviet 5th Army and the 1st Red Banner Army against the border, deploying a crushingly superior force of 12 rifle divisions, 432 Katyushka multiple rocket launchers, 692 tanks and self-propelled guns, and nearly 3,000 mortars and artillery pieces, plus supporting engineers and other specialists.

On the night of August 9th, 1945, Nikolai Krylov, commander of the 5th Army, dispensed with the elaborate artillery preparation planned ahead of the offensive. Instead, his massive force of rifle divisions and tanks moved forward through the pitch-black night, with the sound of the armored vehicles and even gunfire masked by torrential rain. Moving swiftly and attacking furiously, the Soviets overran many Japanese positions before the defenders could muster to repulse them. Many pillboxes and other defenses fell into Russian hands without a shot being fired, their crews huddling in shelters nearby out of the rain. A second wave of infantry with flamethrowers and grenades followed, destroying those strongpoints bypassed by the initial assault.

The Japanese command disintegrated almost immediately under the onslaught. Though the Kwantung Army knew of the attack within an hour of its launch, they learned almost nothing more of its size, location, speed, or objectives during the first day's action as communications broke down. Shiinu desperately ordered the evacuation of Siuyang, including its vital supplies and artillery park, but in the confusion, his soldiers demolished the bridge over the Muleng River before the escape occurred. The Japanese abandoned the supplies and weaponry and fled.

An attempt to rally a second line of resistance met a series of Soviet armored spearheads, moving with the impetus and élan once associated with a panzer division *Schwerpunkt*. The Russians smashed many Japanese units in detail, practically wiping them out or taking them prisoner.

By sunset on August 10th, the Soviets had reached areas they did not expect to seize until August 13th. Meretskov reported tersely, "The 5th Army reached the line of the eastern slopes and main passes of the Huanvotshilin (Hsinhoilin) mountain range, Fantsi (former Kitai Bazar), Laoitsin (inclusive), and Huanfyntai (border post) with its first echelon (two rifle regiments from the first echelon rifle divisions). The army captured the strongly fortified Volynsk center of resistance in the Pogranichnaia Fortified Region and seized trophies (guns, ammunition, warehouses, and prisoners)." (Glantz, 2005, 30).

Meanwhile, the 1st Red Banner Army attacked through the extremely rough terrain of the Pogranichnaya Mountains, held by elements of the Japanese 126th Infantry Division. The Japanese scarcely bothered to garrison this sector of the border, considering the 3,000 foot tall mountains a sufficient deterrent. Nevertheless, the 1st Red Banner Army set about penetrating this "impenetrable" region, not only with infantry, but with 400 tanks and self-propelled guns, which moved over the ridges partly under their own power and partly via manhandling. In addition to the steep crags, the area included thick vegetation, which Colonel-General Afanasy Beloborodov, the army's commander, vividly described: "The mountains were solidly covered with virgin forests of large oaks, cedar, pine, linden and birch, all overgrown with liana and wild grape alternating with creeping brush and underbrush. Thickets filled the spaces between trees, covering the ground like carpets with spines as long as one's finger and strong and sharp as a sewing needle." (Glantz, 2005, 38).

As the 1st Red Banner Army moved into position in the darkness, furious thunderstorms broke over the Pogranichnaya range. Lightning flashed and thunder boomed and echoed deafeningly between the slopes as torrents of rain poured down. Once again, the Soviets decided against preliminary artillery bombardment and attacked under cover of the storm. Caught totally by surprise, the men of the Japanese 126th Infantry Division panicked, running this way and that as the Russians cut them down. In an unsung feat of military maneuver, the Soviets literally broke new roads through the forested mountains. Groups of tanks moved in advance, simply snapping and toppling trees with their steel bulk. Swarms of engineers followed, laboring in the rain-streaked darkness with saws and prime movers, cutting and dragging the fallen trees to form a corduroy road. Following troops worked to improve and widen the new roads as the army advanced through the 19-mile deep band of low mountains.

The Japanese, severely outnumbered, unprepared, and in many cases left without communications as the Soviets cut their telephone lines, collapsed over the course of August 10th. In a few places, small units rallied in defensive positions, holding off the Soviets for several hours before retreating along mountain trails, but in just 50 hours, Beloborodov's men pushed all the way to Pamientung, capturing its bridges across the Maleng river. The 1st Red Banner Army now prepared to make an encircling movement to link up with the Soviet 5th Army deep in Manchurian territory.

The armies on the other fronts struck with similar rapidity and skill, smashing their way deep into Japanese rear areas and making organized resistance impossible. The Soviet 39th Army under Colonel-General Ivan Lyudnikov spearheaded the Trans-Baikal Front, combined with the 6th Guards Tank Army. This force, led by a thousand tanks and other armored vehicles, pushed through the Grand Khingan Mountains between August 10th and 14th, once more confounding Japanese expectations of the range's "impenetrability," albeit at the cost of numerous heat stroke cases in the early part of the offensive due to faulty, easily broken canteens and intense heat in the region of 95 degrees Fahrenheit.

The Soviet 39th Army and other armies forming the Trans-Baikal Front encircled both Japanese field forces and the Halung-Arshaan Fortified Region, in which Kwantung planners put considerable stock. Lyudnikov's engineers built new roads where necessary to bypass the expected lines of advance, totally outmaneuvering the Japanese. In just five days, the Soviets penetrated more than 120 miles into western Manchuria, encircling the Japanese 44th Army and running rampant in the Kwantung rear.

The Battle of Mutanchiang represented one of the only head to head encounters between large Soviet and Japanese forces during the entire operation. The 1st Red Banner Army once more went into action, finally capturing the city of Mutanchiang after heavy fighting. A Japanese account of the toughness of the Red Army T-34/85 medium tanks against the light guns of the Kwantung defense forces still conveys a sense of seething outrage 70 years later: "However, even though the enemy tanks were hit, since the projectiles were not armor piercing, the actual damage was virtually nil. [...] The enemy calmly repaired his tanks on a spot exposed to us. His behavior was arrogant and insolent in the face of our impotence. His tanks remained along the road in column, and avoided the swampy ground nearby. Some of the tank crew members were observed to consist of female as well as male soldiers." (Glantz, 2005, 106).

Although the Japanese soldiers fought bravely wherever they were brought to battle, the Kwantung Army suffered catastrophic defeat at both the strategic and tactical level. Within two weeks, far ahead of the projected schedule, Marshal Vasilevsky's 11 armies drove deep into Manchukuo, enveloping the entire hostile force and forcing its systematic retreat or surrender.

Some of the last fighting occurred in the Kurile Islands off the tip of Kamchatka, where the Japanese managed a few days of resistance due to their highly favorable positions. The Allies agreed that the Kurile Islands would be occupied by U.S. forces, but the Soviet dictator had other ideas: "The actual surrender would not take place for two weeks and, while ordering its forces to cease offensive operations, Japan reserved the right of self-defense. Stalin had long wished to gain control of the Kurils, and decided to seize them before American occupation troops arrived." (Rottman, 2008, 58). In effect, the Soviet Kurile invasion represented a flagrant violation of the Japanese surrender terms in Manchuria, based purely on Stalin's thirst to acquire the island chain regardless of preexisting plans or agreements.

The key portion of the defense fell to the responsibility of Major General Tsutsumi Fusaka, who acquitted himself more successfully than most of the other Kwantung commanders. Major General Alexey Gnechko took a prominent role in the Red Army operation against the Kuriles.

The Soviets launched an amphibious invasion early on August 18th - more than a week after the atomic bomb had been dropped on Nagasaki and days after Japan formally announced surrender - coming ashore through nearly impenetrable fog. The Japanese defenders stood their ground, however, and even counterattacked, inflicting relatively heavy losses. The Soviets reported losing 17 tanks on the first day alone, and an eyewitness described the scene: "Having picked up the noise of motors, the Japanese waited until they could discern the dim outlines of approaching landing-craft before unleashing a hail of lead. [...] Gnechko's first wave wilted. Thirteen landing-craft full of troops sank or exploded. Others burst into flames, illuminating the flailing occupants, many of whom leapt into the strait's treacherous currents and disappeared." (Glantz, 2005, 281).

The Japanese batteries proved troublesome for the Soviet ships to knock out. The Russian gunners found sighting nearly impossible in the thick fog, while the Japanese enjoyed the "home turf" advantage of pre-designated aiming points. Furthermore, the IJA placed their batteries in grottoes, which afforded excellent protection. On August 19th, Soviet sapper teams successfully crawled forward and placed enough explosives around the two main batteries on Shumshir Island to blow them to pieces.

The Japanese capitulated on August 19th, but fierce fighting erupted again almost immediately, with each side blaming the other. Combat continued for the next two days, with the Japanese launching an attack of 20 tanks (destroyed by Soviet anti-tank guns) and the war's final kamikaze attack scoring a hit on a Russian destroyer. A second Japanese armor attack involving 18 tanks also failed, though it inflicted considerable losses in killed and wounded on the Soviets.

Finally, on August 21st, Tsutsumi capitulated to the Soviets again. This time, the surrender held, and over the next two days the Red Army soldiers took 14,800 IJA troops into custody on Shumshir.

This final victory broke the will of the Japanese in the Kurile Islands to resist. The Soviets swept through the island chain between August 23rd and August 29th, meeting basically no hostile action. The collapse of Japanese morale yielded 91,550 prisoners to the Soviets, including 16 Kwantung Army generals. The Soviets claimed a total cost to their side of 290 KIA or MIA, plus nearly 400 wounded, but the actual figures likely ranged higher (though not as high as the Japanese estimate of 2,500 KIA and 3,000 WIA, which would have practically decimated Gnechko's 8,000-man force outright).

The Soviets also pushed into the Korean peninsula, retaking it from the Japanese who had controlled it since 1910. They chose a leader for the Koreans from among trusted communists of Korean origin – a man named Kim Il-Sung, whose descendants continue to rule North Korea's "Hermit Kingdom" into the 21st century.

As a result of the Soviet offensive, a grim fate awaited most of the Japanese resettled to Manchuria during the previous decade and a half. The Red Army conducted a reign of terror in the defeated territories, plundering, raping, burning, and killing – though some modern Russian historians dispute this. The Japanese frequently proved their own worst enemies, however, with mass suicide and massacres claiming large percentages of settlers.

Though charged with bringing as many settlers out of Manchuria as possible, the Kwantung Army soldiers tended to view Japanese refugees as obstacles to their own escape and evacuation. Showing the same murderous brutality towards their own people as they frequently exhibited towards foreigners, the Kwantung troops mowed down the civilians given into their charge. Tanaka Toshiko survived such an event: "[A]t night, the soldiers suddenly began summary shooting of the evacuees. [...] She remained alive among the piles of dead bodies. Thinking that all the settlers were dead, the Japanese soldiers left in a hurry. [...] Only decades later did she figure out that the soldiers shot them because the women and children were in the way of their repatriation." (Itoh, 2010, 32).

Japanese settlers often committed mass suicide in preference to meeting their deaths at the hands of their enemies, a kind of self-immolation characteristic of traditional Japanese culture. In these killings, the women and children typically took a passive role, raising the question of their actual willingness to die. The inhabitants of a village or town gathered together, and then the men killed their wives and children with samurai swords, bayonets, and whatever firearms they owned. In some cases, women strangled their infants before submitting to execution. After killing their families, the Japanese men then usually committed suicide or killed each other in pairs, simultaneously shooting or stabbing each other to death. Sometimes, husbands and wives killed each other or took cyanide pills together. While some people survived the mass suicides, they rarely did so without wounds, which made their subsequent survival even more difficult.

The Red Army committed a number of large-scale massacres themselves, in addition to hundreds of random killings. Suzuki Noriko, a schoolteacher, witnessed one such murder after surviving a series of mass suicides, Chinese attacks, and massacres: "As she hid in the maize field alone, a Soviet Army truck stopped [...] Russiansoldiers took a young Japanese woman into the truck and took her clothes off. Then she heard the woman's screams. She was being subjected to gang rape. [Soon] they threw her away on the road. Suzuki heard Russian female soldiers laughing in high-pitched tones at the woman. The truck [...] drove over her body and left." (Itoh, 2010, 34).

Full on massacres occurred at several sites, and one of the most notorious occurred during the "Gegenmiao Incident" at Gegenmiao Lamasery. 1,800 Japanese women and children sought sanctuary in the lamasery, but Soviet soldiers and Chinese townspeople dragged them out. The Soviets shot and bayoneted many, crushing others under the treads of their tanks. Both Soviet soldiers and Chinese men raped the more attractive women before killing them. The vengeful Chinese used knives or clubs on their victims, and drove hundreds into the river, where they drowned.

That autumn, the Soviets herded thousands of captured settlers into the abandoned town of Fangzheng, interning them there over the winter. With little food available, approximately 3,000 of these prisoners died from starvation and cold.

At other times, individual Red Army troopers or small Soviet units showed the reserved, practical compassion of soldiers towards the defeated Japanese civilians. One Japanese woman, then a small child, later recalled how she sat crying beside her mother's corpse at the roadside. A passing squad of Soviets in a truck stopped, picked her up, and drove her to a town. There they located a woman willing to adopt the orphaned Japanese girl before driving on their way, thus preventing her from dying of thirst and hunger.

With the Russians in the territory, the Chinese themselves attacked the columns of Japanese civilians attempting to reach safety in large towns or at the coast. Using an assortment of weapons, the Chinese harried these groups of Japanese, picking them off singly or sometimes closing in to slaughter them in hundreds. Japanese children, if they survived mass suicide and IJA massacres, fared somewhat better than adults in terms of survival. The Chinese peasants adopted many of the younger children, particularly in the case of infertile women who wanted a child or children of their own, or families with all daughters (adopting a Japanese boy) or all sons (adopting a Japanese girl). That said, some Chinese killed Japanese children they found or simply left them to perish, and on other occasions, Chinese seized children from unwilling mothers in order to sell them to other Chinese. Realizing that childless Chinese families wanted children, many of the Japanese women who guessed they would soon die gave their children to Chinese at the roadside or left them in the field next to a village, hoping to secure their survival in this fashion.

By the time the war was over, of the 270,000 Japanese civilian settlers in Manchuria, approximately 44% died, 52% returned home to Japan in the following months and years, and the balance remained in China, willingly or unwillingly. 1,010,000 Japanese also received repatriation from other parts of the former empire by the end of 1946, though approximately 5 million remained. The Japanese government worked secretly to prevent their return, hoping to avoid the necessity of feeding or housing them, and in some cases even trying to offer these people as "laborers" to their former colonial subjects in place of cash reparations.

Togo Shigenori spearheaded this initiative, but mass repatriation eventually occurred largely due to the initiative of President Truman. Already turning his eyes towards the next conflict, the president wanted a stable China, figuring it would be less likely to turn communist, and thus viewed the Japanese expatriates as economically and socially destabilizing. Thus, during 1946 and 1947, American Navy ships carried millions of Japanese back to the homeland which had effectively abandoned them, leaving tens of thousands behind. In contrast to the Chinese adoption of at least some Japanese children, the Japanese performed forced abortions on most of the pregnant women who came back, ensuring that the repatriated women bore few babies with Russian or Chinese fathers.

In sum, the Japanese invasion of Manchuria and establishment of Manchukuo represented both part of Japan's development into a modern state and the genesis of World War II's Pacific Theater. China, Russia, and Japan all wanted Manchuria in the first years of the 20th century due to their respective ambitions to enter the modern, industrial age and the resources this northeast Chinese region offered.

Russia's loss to Japan in the Russo-Japanese War of 1904-1905, followed by the internal chaos attendant on the Russian Revolution of 1917 and the ensuing Russian Civil War, had removed one of the potential players from the board during a crucial span of nearly three decades. China disintegrated into a period of civil strife also, as Imperial, republican, and eventually Nationalist and communist factions emerged to battle alongside swarms of grand or petty warlords, each attempting to build local empires. As the only one of the three competitors sufficiently united and organized at the time, Japan naturally, perhaps inevitably, took Manchuria. The economic windfall provided by the territory, combined with Japan's relatively fast abandonment of the gold standard, enabled a swift rebound in Japanese fortunes in the early 1930s.

Like all pivotal moments in history, the Japanese invasion offers a tantalizing spectrum of "what ifs." In particular, it is possible to wonder what would have happened if the Japanese had elected to consolidate their gains, content themselves with the economically lucrative holdings of Manchukuo, Korea, and Taiwan, and seek normalized relations with the rest of the world. Instead, of course, the military ran completely out of control, using the precious resources gained to fund an ultimately suicidal rush to boundless dominion. It would take another decade, but the Imperial Japanese Army learned the limits of its strength against the fleets, shells, and bombs of Britain and the United States.

Perhaps fittingly, Manchuria, the starting line for Japan's imperial adventure, left the nation's control in an even more spectacular fashion than it first entered it. The Soviet Red Army destroyed the once-powerful Kwantung Army in just two weeks with the final blitzkrieg of World War II, demonstrating its own emergence as a thoroughly professional modern military force in the process. In the end, the Empire of the Rising Sun's return to the scene of its 1905 tragedies and successes led chiefly to tens of thousands more Japanese, along with Chinese, Manchus, and Soviets, sleeping under the stones of a lonely field illuminated by "the red setting sun of distant Manchuria."

Online Resources

Other World War II titles by Charles River Editors

Other titles about the invasion of Manchuria on Amazon

Bibliography

Bergamini, David. *Japan's Imperial Conspiracy.* New York, 1971.

Birnbaum, Phyllis. *Manchu princess, Japanese spy: the story of Kawashima Yoshiko, the cross- dressing spy who commanded her own army.* New York, 2015.

Coox, Alvin D. *Nomonhan: Japan Against Russia, 1939.* Stanford, 1985.

Glantz, David M. *Soviet Operational and Tactical Combat in Manchuria, 1945: 'August Storm.'* London, 2005.

Guderian, Heinz and Constantine Fitzgibbon (translator). *Panzer Leader.* New York, 1964.

Hata, Ikuhiko, and Alvin D. Coox (translator). "Continental expansion, 1905-1941." *The Cambridge History of Japan: Volume 6, The Twentieth Century.* Cambridge, 2008.

Itoh, Mayumi. *Japanese War Orphans in Manchuria: Forgotten Victims of World War II.* New York, 2010.

Ogata, Sadako N. *Defiance in Manchuria: The Making of Japanese Foreign Policy, 1931-1932.* Berkeley and Los Angeles, 1964.

Paine, S.C.M. *The Wars for Asia, 1911-1949.* Cambridge, 2012.

Puyi, Henry. *The Last Manchu: The Autobiography of Henry Pu Yi, Last Emperor of China.* New York, 2010.

Rottman, Gordon L. and Akira Takizawa. *World War II Japanese Tank Tactics.* Oxford, 2008.

Sella, Amnon. "Khalkhin-gol: The Forgotten War". *Journal of Contemporary History* 18.4 (1983): 651–687.

Smith, Norman. *Intoxicating Manchuria: Alcohol, Opium, and Culture in China's Northeast.* Vancouver, 2012.

Sydney Morning Herald, The. *Manchuria. Ma Chan-Shan's Offensive. Battle Near Tsitsihar.* Thursday, November 19th, 1931 issue, page 9.

Young, Louise. *Japan's Total Empire: Manchuria and the Culture of Wartime Imperialism.* Berkeley and Los Angeles, 1998.

The Rape of Nanking

Chapter 1: The Military Prelude to the Nanking Massacre

Japanese imperialism on the Asian mainland began long before the usually recognized start of World War II. Following Admiral Perry's expedition to open the xenophobic Tokugawa Shogunate to foreign trade in 1852, the Japanese rapidly adopted new technologies and used them to impose their will on the neighboring Asian mainland. For the second time in history, Japan exerted its dominance over Korea, then clashed with China in 1894 over the Korean question. The Japanese decisively defeated the backward and moribund Chinese imperial navy and imposed a victor's treaty.

Tokugawa Clan Crest

The Japanese next directed their aggression, successfully, against the Russians in the 1905 Russo-Japanese war. Though the Japanese observed the rules of "civilized warfare" punctiliously during the conflict, the fierce, utterly mercilessly warrior culture of the samurai lurked just beneath the surface, waiting to emerge in the coming decades.

The doom of Nanking emerged from the collision between seemingly endless civil war that swept China from 1911 until well after the end of World War II, killing approximately 20 million people, and Japanese imperial ambitions in Manchuria in the 1930s. The Japanese had all the hallmarks of a major maritime power, similar to Great Britain or the United States of America, yet decided to develop their land forces and fight large-scale land wars, discarding the advantages of a focus on oceanic strategy.

Seeking economic independence and the resources needed to continue their modernization as a twentieth century military power, the Japanese manufactured a transparent pretext in 1931 and attacked northern China, exploiting the ongoing bloodbath between the Chinese Nationalists and Communists:

"On 18 September 1931 Japan launched a full-scale invasion of Manchuria in response to an explosion near Shenyang, bending a few meters of its railway track, which it repaired by 6 a.m. the following day. [...] Although the Japanese government accused the Chinese of perpetrating the vandalism, before long its own internal investigation held members of the Japanese army responsible." (Paine, 2012, 13).

The Japanese characterized this massive onslaught as an "Incident," for a very simple reason. Many of Japan's supplies came from the United States, as did those of the Chinese. The U.S. Neutrality Act forbade selling anything to countries engaged in aggressive war. The Japanese used the term "incident" as a legalistic euphemism for their war, thus enabling them to continue trading with U.S. businesses, at least temporarily.

Manchuria represented a rich prize for the hungrily expansionist Japanese, supplying China with most of its oil, gold, and iron, and accounting for around a third of the entire nation's economic activity. This undefended economic powerhouse quickly fell to the Japanese "Kanto Army," which, bizarrely, set up "Henri Puyi," the deposed Chinese emperor, as the emperor of the new puppet state of Manchukuo.

The Japanese civil government attempted to reign in the ascendant military, but met with assassinations and broader expulsion of several cabinets in response. The Japanese attacked Shanghai, the center of foreign investment, in 1932, in an effort to coerce the Chinese into accepting the "independence" of Manchukuo, or "Land of the Manchus." The Imperial government offered, in effect, to trade Shanghai back to the Chinese in exchange for official recognition of their puppet state. This scheme backfired, enraging the Chinese and briefly uniting many of them behind the Nationalist leader Chiang Kai-Shek.

The Japanese developed Manchuria economically, transforming it into a relatively modern industrial powerhouse filled with mines and factories. Manchuria furnished the dynamo permitting the Japanese war machine to continue functioning.

The Manchurians themselves earned approximately 150% of the money received by the highest-paid industrial workers elsewhere in China, yet this did not translate into a higher standard of living. The Japanese siphoned off almost all production for their own uses, leading to a profound lack of consumer goods and a local economy providing only basic necessities. The Japanese economy, meanwhile, boomed, recovering swiftly from the worldwide Great Depression of the 1930s, a disaster caused by the survival of the antiquated gold standard in an era of economic transformation.

The Japanese, however, continued their aggression, steadily seizing additional provinces to add to their prize. They left the League of Nations in 1933 in response to that body's condemnation of their actions. In part, their demographic explosion provided the impetus to expansionism, with a population that rose from 30 million to 65 million in the course of just a few generations. Hashimoto Kingoro, a Lieutenant Colonel, wrote:

"There are only three ways left to Japan to escape from the pressures of surplus population... emigration, advance into world markets, and expansion of territory. The first door, emigration, has been barred to us by the anti-Japanese immigration policies of other countries. The second door... is being pushed shut by tariff barriers and the abrogation of commercial treaties. What should Japan do when two of the three doors have been closed against her?" (Chang, 1997, 26-27).

Of course, the Japanese made conditions much more difficult for themselves due to their naked brutality, which appalled even the most profit-minded foreign business owners, and their inability to stop. Had they consolidated their gains in Manchukuo and worked to build its economic strength alongside that of Japan, their involvement in later warfare, including the catastrophic defeat in World War II, might well have been avoided.

During the mid-1930s, Chiang Kai-Shek believed the Japanese too strong and too entrenched in Manchuria to oust with the forces available to China. Instead, he concentrated on his war against the communists, using a gradual strategy in which an army of 800,000 men moved forward into communist territory, constructing a network of blockhouses as they went to control the countryside. Chiang Kai-Shek signed the Tanggu Truce with the Japanese in mid-1933 to buy himself time, causing them to withdraw north of the Great Wall of China.

Chiang Kai-Shek

The Tanggu Truce proved nearly worthless and the Japanese seized not only Mongolia, but also resumed advances south of the Great Wall as soon as they created pretexts that seemed adequate to them. The Japanese turned Mongolia into "Mengkukuo," under a puppet ruler descended from Genghis Khan himself and bearing a name that would not be out of place in "Gulliver's Travels" – Demchugdongrub.

Chapter 2: The Second Sino-Japanese War in 1937

Chiang Kai-Shek, later scorned due to associations with fascist leaders he, in fact, largely despised, led his Nationalists in a highly successful series of reforms in 1935, 1936, and early 1937. The Nationalists jettisoned the destructive silver standard, with its extreme volatility (second only to the gold standard for economic harmfulness), and instituted a widespread program of rural credit to rescue farmers from the effects of the long civil war.

Tax reforms eliminated unnecessary burdens and the Chinese economy expanded vigorously. A full recovery did not occur, but it never had a chance to – no economic program could fully restore a huge, complex country battered by 25 years of civil war in just two years, and later criticisms appear objectively unfair to the Nationalists.

De facto, the Second Sino-Japanese War began in 1931 when the Japanese invaded and occupied Manchuria and created their puppet state of Manchukuo. However, 1937 still represents a change in the pattern of conflict as the piecemeal advance of the Japanese army grew into a juggernaut-like onrush that disregarded all previous agreements with Chiang Kai-Shek. Chiang's policy of dealing with the crippling internal struggle first, then with the Japanese once China unified, foundered on the rock of events outside his control.

The fatal breach occurred on the night of July 7th, 1937, a confluence of three "7s" particularly ominous in Chinese numerology. The night, hot and brilliantly illuminated by a full moon, prompted a Japanese unit stationed near the Yongding River's Marco Polo Bridge to carry out night exercises. During the maneuvers, one Japanese soldier went missing, and portions of his unit crossed the Marco Polo Bridge to the Chinese side, ostensibly to look for him.

The soldier soon appeared, unharmed, but the Chinese soldiers from the 29th Army saw Japanese riflemen on their side of the river and opened fire. A short firefight ensued that ended with the Japanese retreating. The Japanese company commander called his Chinese counterpart by telephone and apologized, and the Chinese officer responded in a similar manner, both men seeking avoidance of another "incident."

The Japanese officer's immediate superior, however – the man in charge of the brigade – had less pacific intentions. He ordered the artillery at his disposal to bombard the Chinese headquarters and barracks on the other side of the Yongding River. As shells plowed through walls and tore apart men's bodies with blasts of shrapnel, the Chinese commander, goaded past any caution, ordered the batteries available to him to return fire, resulting in a vicious artillery duel.

Yongding River, under the Marco Polo Bridge. Photo by Fanghong.

The Japanese responded by moving hundreds of thousands of soldiers to attack southward and confront the "atrocious" Chinese army. The communist Mao Zedong publicly pretended to offer support to Chiang Kai-Shek and the Nationalists, but secretly plotted treachery, intending to leave the Nationalists and Japanese to maul each other so that his Red Army could pick up the pieces:

> "On July 31, however, showing his intention to avoid serious combat with the Japanese, Mao radioed his military lieutenants that the previous order was for propaganda purposes. In reality, he said, the troops should move slowly. In particular, they could 'move 50 li [500 meters] each day, and pause one day after every three days.'" (Taylor, 2009, 147).

Mao Zedong

    The Japanese invaded Hebei Province first. Soon, China and Korea hosted no less than 21 Japanese divisions. The Chinese fought back, and, though the Japanese ultimately overwhelmed them and drove them back, the victory came at a high price. Around 100,000 Japanese soldiers suffered injury or death by the end of 1937, with the war destined to continue even more viciously for years, lasting into the 1940s.

    Chiang Kai-Shek attempted to halt the Japanese at Shanghai, both for reasons of national prestige and in the hope of drawing the western powers into the struggle on his side. Thousands of foreigners lived in the rich trading port and immense business interests from Europe and the United States maintained important branches there. The Shanghai campaign began on August 11th, when the Nationalist air force attempted to bomb the Japanese warships in Shanghai harbor but instead, incompetently, struck the city's main foreign quarter, killing more than 1,300 foreign civilians.

The Nationalists mustered more than half a million military personnel (including air crews and support units) during their counterattack on Shanghai. Street fighting began on August 13th and initially the Chinese forced the Japanese marines back to a precarious foothold on the city wharves. However, the Japanese soon put 75,000 more men ashore. In brutal fighting in the streets and along the Whangpoo riverbank, the Japanese pushed the Chinese steadily back, albeit while sustaining thousands of wounded and dead.

At this pivotal juncture, even Zhou Enlai urged Mao to commit the communist Chinese Red Army forces to the struggle, fighting alongside their Nationalist counterparts against the common enemy of their nation. Coldly, Mao refused, preferring to see hundreds of thousands of Chinese die and extensive new territories fall under Japanese control if this raised the odds of his eventually defeating Chiang Kai-Shek. Mao called this the "Defeat for All" strategy.

On November 5th, 1937, the Japanese played their trump card. Intelligence reports indicated Chiang Kai-Shek – to his later open regret – withdrew the men guarding Hangzhou Bay on Shanghai's southern flank. One hundred warships from the Imperial Japanese Navy (IJN) 4th Fleet put three divisions, the 6th Kumamoto Division, the 114th Utsunomiya Division, and the 18th Kurume Division, ashore in Hangzhou Bay.

This force, known as the Japanese 10th Army, drove northward, trying to cut off Chiang Kai-Shek's men in a salient bounded by their lines to the west, the Yangtze River to the north, and the other Japanese forces (and the ocean) to the east and south. The Japanese used balloon-based propaganda to exaggerate the numbers of this force and terrorize the men risking being trapped in Shanghai, as a Japanese newspaper reported:

> "At noon on the 6th, a large advertising balloon unfolded and floated high in the skies over the north bank of the Suzhou River, and at the same time a great war cry suddenly arose from our troops. Look! Can you not clearly read what is written on the balloon floating lazily in the low rain clouds south of the Yangtze River? 'One million Japanese troops land north of Hangzhou Bay.'" (Honda, 2015, 9).

Regardless of the overblown figure of one million Japanese soldiers (which would require 10,000 men squeezed onto each warship, besides being more than Japan had under arms in 1937), deadly peril threatened the Nationalist Chinese soldiers. A very real possibility of encirclement loomed, after which massacre would inevitably ensue. Chiang Kai-Shek ordered a retreat on November 8th, but not before his corps of 30,000 young officers sustained 70% casualties and his army suffered 187,000 soldiers WIA or KIA.

Chapter 3: The Battle of Nanking

Having ejected the Chinese from Shanghai at a cost of 9,115 deaths and 31,257 WIA, the Japanese pressed their advantage by following the fleeing Nationalist forces towards their capital of Nanking. The Japanese military also fanned out to snap up a number of key provincial capitals while the Chinese remained off balance following their defeat.

A German named Horst Baerensprung left a vivid account of the retreating Nationalists marching through the winter rain:

> "From a suburb of Nanking, I watched for almost seven hours as troops passed along the rutted muddy road. […] Even most of the officers were on foot […] The rain whipped at them mercilessly, incessantly […] The clouds hung so low that you could almost grab hold of them. The Purple Mountain and Lion Hill, the hallmarks of Nanking, were lost in fog. […] I looked at these carefully wrapped machine guns and then at those soldiers, who were soaked to the bone […] Christ was probably thinking of times like these when he advised his disciples: 'He that hath no sword, let him sell his garment and buy one.'" (Rabe, 1998, 24).

The Battle of Nanking began on December 1st, 1937. Chiang Kai-Shek, in his embattled capital, took overall command of the forces remaining at his disposal. In desperation, Chiang appealed to the Russian dictator Josef Stalin for Soviet troops to aid in throwing back the Japanese. Stalin responded that if he entered the conflict, the western powers might view him as victimizing Japan and enter the war against him. However, he did continue to send tanks, aircraft, and other military vehicles to the Nationalists, offering the support to the front-line Chinese that his fellow communist Mao denied.

Defending the sturdy walls of the city, and manning a series of pillboxes with interlocking fields of fire, the Chinese fought for days with dogged courage. The crack 88th Division died almost to a man, along with its senior officers, but took 566 Japanese KIA with them and wounded more than 1,500 additional soldiers. The Japanese, however, possessed superior weapons, plus better training than most (though not all) of the Chinese divisions. Using heavy artillery, the Japanese slowly battered the defenses to pieces, leveling part of the city and setting other portions ablaze.

Chiang Kai-Shek and his wife left the city by air on December 7th, while the reformed warlord Tang Shengzhi remained willingly to fight a rearguard action. Finally, on December 12th, the suicidal courage of Japanese soldiers with bamboo ladders enabled them to take the Zhonghua Gate in Nanking's walls. At the same time, a unit of tanks crashed through the Shuixi Gate and burst into the city.

Tang Shengzhi

    Tang Shengzhi ordered the remaining soldiers to break out. Thousands died, drowning in the Yangtze, shot by the Japanese, or trampled to death by their comrades attempting to force their way out of the single gate not yet in Japanese hands. Some 70,000 men of the Nationalist army lost their lives in the Battle of Nanking. Tang himself escaped in a coal-driven boat with a few of his leading officers.

    The Japanese hoped the Chinese would surrender following the loss of their capital. Instead, Chiang Kai-Shek issued a fire-breathing statement widely distributed in China, which, in large measure, struck exactly the chord the Nationalist leader hoped it would:

    "'The war will not be decided in Nanking or any other city,' he said. 'It will be decided in the countryside of our vast country and by the inflexible will of our people. We shall fight on every step of the way, and every inch of the 40,000,000 square *li* of our territory.'" (Taylor, 2009, 152).

China, as Chiang Kai-Shek hoped, would fight on against the Japanese, though the Nationalist cause suffered a serious blow from the decimation of its soldiery. However, the date also marked the beginning of one of history's most concentrated atrocities.

Chapter 4: The Start of the Nanking Massacre

The Japanese showed a profound lack of understanding of human psychology during their advance after the seizure of Shanghai, compounded by a Bushido ethic and sense of racial superiority that together gave license – in fact, extreme encouragement – to sadistic brutality and murderous impulses. They believed that killing and torturing the Chinese in vast numbers would cow the rest into submission.

Japanese Soldiers Marching to Nanking

Instead, their deeds predictably produced rage, hatred, and iron determination in their adversaries, and united disparate Chinese factions with a shared resolve to resist the Japanese and make their conquest of China as difficult and costly as possible.

Nevertheless, the Japanese never grasped this fundamental and fairly evident truth. Chinese intransigence in the face of Japanese brutality simply led the Japanese to believe they had not used *enough* cruelty and caused them to expand the butchery further. In the primly evasive phrase of Emperor Hirohito, the Japanese wanted these measures to produce "self-reflection" among the Chinese.

While Japanese leaders gave no specific order for the Nanking Massacre, they explicitly commanded the literal extermination of the Chinese peasantry during the march from Shanghai to Nanking:

> "All the law-abiding people have retreated within the walls. Treat everyone found outside the walls as anti-Japanese and destroy them. [...] Since it is convenient in conducting sweep operations to burn down houses, prepare materials." (Bix, 2000, 333).

The Japanese 10th Army carried out these orders assiduously, giving a preview of the hecatomb to follow once Nanking fell. The Japanese soldiers shot Chinese military prisoners *en masse*, or, in a number of cases, roped large numbers of wounded Chinese together, drenched them in gasoline, and set them on fire to burn agonizingly alive. They also burned down every village and small city they encountered and raped practically every woman or female child seized.

Panicked masses of Chinese farmers and townspeople flowed across the landscape ahead of the Japanese advance, desperately seeking escape. Many sought refuge inside Nanking, destined to become a trap where tens of thousands of them would die lingering, painful deaths and then be discarded in the river or "Trenches of Ten Thousand Corpses."

These actions represented no anomaly from historic Japanese behavior. Though Bushido represented a code of "honor" in the same way as European chivalry, its focus remained tremendously different. The chivalric codes of Europe contained injunctions to spare (or even defend) the weak and defenseless, to show mercy to prisoners and the wounded, and so forth. Though flouted at times, these codes slowly evolved into the later code of "gentleman's warfare" and eventually into the Geneva Convention, which effectively remains the chivalric code in an updated, legalistic format.

Bushido, on the other hand, emphasized success as honorable and failure as dishonorable, which explains why defeated Japanese, for centuries, committed seppuku rather than survive in "shame." The dark corollary of this grim practice expressed itself in active hatred and aggression towards those who would not or could not fight. Not merely dismissed as "unworthy," they drew venomous loathing from the Japanese under arms.

To the Japanese, the concepts of an honorably defeated prisoner or a noncombatant did not exist. A fighting man who, outnumbered, exhausted, wounded, and hopeless, chose to surrender did not represent a fellow warrior deserving a measure of sympathy for misfortune due to circumstances far beyond his individual control. He represented, instead, a loathsome criminal and a sort of traitor to the concept of the fighting man, deserving punishment for not killing himself in defeat.

Worse, this loathing extended to noncombatants; the Japanese, preparing for the invasion of the home islands by the Americans in 1945, trained their children in the thousands to use grenades so that they could pull the pin, walk up to Americans, and detonate the weapon, killing themselves and perhaps one or more soldiers as well.

The reflexes of Bushido trained men to see even a civilian who failed to immolate themselves for their nation as a sort of abomination, a renegade deserving only contempt, pain, and death. This frenzied code produced a capacity for boundless cruelty without remorse or any kind of introspection, particularly when coupled with the fascist-style nationalism of the 20th century Japanese military.

Almost precisely the same behavior manifested itself during the Japanese invasion of Korea in 1592, some 350 years earlier. The Japanese samurai acted the same as their remote descendants in Nanking, killing tens of thousands of civilians, committing mass torture and mass rape, burning countless buildings, and time and again showing in their own accounts evidence of a deep relish and pleasure derived from witnessing the torment and killing of thousands of other human beings:

> "Some Japanese accounts note the taking of 20,000 heads at Chinju. Korean records claim 60,000 deaths, and both figures imply a massacre of soldiers and non-combatants alike. [...] That night, while the Nam river downstream from the castle walls flowed red, and headless corpses still choked its banks, the victorious Japanese generals celebrated in the Ch'oksongnu Pavilion, from which the best view of this hellish scene could be appreciated." (Turnbull, 2002, 160).

Japanese scroll paintings and woodcuts of the 1592 invasion frankly include numerous scenes eerily reminiscent of the horrors photographed by stunned foreigners in Nanking three and a half centuries later: soldiers cutting down fleeing, screaming civilians and setting fire to their homes, grinning soldiers dragging women away to be raped, female corpses sprawled on the ground with their skirts ominously pulled up to expose their lower bodies, presumably indicating the Japanese raped and then murdered them.

The Japanese cut off 214,752 heads during their invasion, not counting those discarded as being of "low quality," and shipped an additional 38,000 Korean noses, severed and pickled, back to Japan as a trophy. The Japanese buried these pitiful remnants in the misnamed

"Mimizuka," or "Ear Mound," which still stands in Kyoto. The Shogun Toyotomi Hideyoshi gave orders to his samurai which would have fit naturally with the men who committed the Nanking Massacre twelve generations later:

> "Mow down everyone universally, without discriminating between young and old, men and women, clergy and the laity – high ranking soldiers on the battlefield, that goes without saying, but also the hill folk, down to the poorest and meanest and send the heads to Japan." (Hawley, 2005, 465-466).

A gentle and humane Japanese Buddhist monk named Keinen accompanied Hideyoshi's expedition, and recorded an endless catalog of horrors. He saw men and women tortured and killed in front of their children, workmen beaten to death, samurai butchering villagers, and countless slaves led away in iron and bamboo collars.

He also walked through towns and into the countryside beyond and found the ground carpeted for some distance with the mutilated corpses of slaughtered Koreans that he could not, in his own words, "force himself to look at." Finally, in despair, he attempted to sum up his feelings with a stark phrase suitable for the epitaph of Nanking centuries after his death, as the samurai of another age spread similar desolation in China: "Hell cannot be in any other place except here." (Turnbull, 2002, 206).

In a real sense, the soldiers who raped, tortured, and killed hundreds of thousands of civilians in Nanking simply carried on the long-standing traditions of samurai warfare. Some Japanese, of course, remained untouched by this brutal code of "honor" and showed compassion. But in the Rape of Nanking, their numbers proved to be a very small minority, to the misfortune of those caught in the Japanese Army's clutches.

Chapter 5: Foreigners Prepare the Safety Zone

Very few foreigners remained in Nanking at the time of its fall, but that tiny handful made a tremendous difference in the outcome. Many more Chinese would likely have died without these courageous two dozen Europeans, who enjoyed nearly complete immunity due to the Japanese wish to avoid bringing the wrath of the western powers down on their heads at this crucial juncture.

The majority of this group consisted of Americans, and since at this point the United States still supplied many materials to the Japanese, killing or detaining these people would be impolitic at best and disastrous at worst. Most participated in missionary work, while one, John Rabe, represented the German Siemens company in the city and performed many acts of heroic kindness despite his status as an avowed Nazi (albeit one focusing almost exclusively on the "socialist" aspects of the NSDAP rather than on its militant or racist facets).

As the Japanese pushed the Nationalists out of Shanghai, the foreigners banded together to create a "Safety Zone" in the western quadrant of the city. At this point, they feared violence and rape from Chiang Kai-Shek's nationalist soldiers, disorganized and undisciplined following defeat, as the missionaries imagined them. Naively, they imagined that the Safety Zone would exist for only a few days, providing the local Chinese with shelter from their compatriots under arms. Then, when the civilized, honorable, and disciplined Japanese arrived, the foreigners could allow everyone to return home safely.

Though the exact opposite of reality – the Chinese soldiers proved too busy fighting for their lives to create the type of mayhem feared, and still retained some of their discipline, while the Japanese approached along roads they strewed with raped and shattered bodies – this scenario at least served to motivate the foreigners to prepare the Safety Zone quickly and thoroughly before the Japanese entered the city:

> "Indeed, one of the foreign eyewitnesses of the 1937 massacre admitted: "We were more prepared for excesses from the fleeing Chinese... but never, never from the Japanese. On the contrary, we had expected that with the appearance of the Japanese the return of peace, quiet, and prosperity would occur." (Chang, 1997, 83).

Many foreigners fled immediately before fighting reached Nanking, leaving only a resolute core of those willing to help in any way they could. Some of the last to escape prior to the Rape left on American gunboats. One of these, the *Panay*, suffered the grimly ironic fate of sinking at the hands of Japanese pilots – its occupants would actually have found more safety in the city they abandoned than in the vessel in which they departed.

Attacking an American gunboat represented a stark departure from overall Japanese policy at the time, which generally treated all European and American foreigners as sacrosanct. Unusually for a military establishment where questioning an order frequently led to summary execution, the Japanese pilots protested the orders to attack the *Panay* repeatedly and vehemently.

Only after several rounds of threats from their officers did they reluctantly bomb and strafe the vessel. This appears to be an indication that a splinter, reckless military faction actually ordered the attack, rather than the main command structure.

The remaining group consisted of 17 U.S. citizens, six Germans, two Russians, a Britisher, and an Austrian. These men and women devised the idea of a Safety Zone in November, approximately a month before the Japanese took the city, and organized themselves into the International Committee for the Nanking Safety Zone during their first official meeting on November 22nd, 1937. At this gathering, the 27 Committee members also elected John Rabe as their chairman.

Rabe, a small, bald, bespectacled man with a thick cookie duster mustache and a disarming sense of humor alongside an explosive temper when confronted by injustice or disorder, had returned to the city to represent Siemens' interests and look after his own property when he learned of Japanese bombing. He stated in his diary that he had no wish to die for either, but felt he could not leave the city anyway: "Under such circumstances, can I, may I, cut and run? I don't think so. Anyone who has ever sat in a dugout and held a trembling Chinese child in each hand through the long hours of an air raid can understand what I feel." (Rabe, 1998, 5).

Rabe began his humanitarian work in Nanking in an effort to help his 30 Chinese servants, most of whose homes lay in the Japanese-controlled north and who could not now return home through the fighting lines. He made a primitive dugout to shelter from shrapnel during air raids, stocked food and water, and even prepared vinegar masks to try to preserve his life and the lives of his employees if the Japanese used poison gas. As it happened, the Japanese used gas 13 times during the Battle of Nanking, but abandoned the practice long before the city fell because the vapors frequently blew back into their lines and killed many of their own soldiers.

Rabe also painted a huge swastika on a piece of canvas 20 feet across and placed it flat on the ground outside his house, so that the Japanese pilots would hopefully identify it as a German residence and refrain from bombing it. With unintentional understatement – considering that the Safety Zone might have saved as many as 50,000 lives – Rabe reported tersely on his November 22nd election as Committee chairman:

"Five p.m. meeting of the International Committee for Establishing a Neutral Zone for Noncombatants in Nanking. They elect me chairman. My protests are to no avail. I give in for the sake of a good cause. I hope I prove worthy of the post, which can very well become important." (Rabe, 1998, 27).

As the Japanese began their attack, all of the Chinese residents with enough money to flee left the city, leaving behind the poorest people to suffer whatever fate might bring them. Rabe, confronted by a Nationalist colonel named Huang who berated him for creating a Safety Zone when the remaining civilians, trapped with nowhere to go, might otherwise be coerced into aiding his soldiers, asked in disgust why the rich always demand that those most unfortunate in life serve as martyrs to their country while the affluent escape, heaping scorn on those who die for them.

The International Committee worked feverishly to set up the Safety Zone with whatever materials they could access. The Zone covered a significant area in the western part of Nanking, forming a stretched hexagon bounded by major roads – North Chungshan Road on the north, Chung Yang Road on the east, Hanchung Road on the south, and part of Haikang Road on the west.

The Zone included the American, German, and Japanese embassies, several missionary-operated universities including the University of Nanking, the Drum Tower Hospital, and the Army Staff College, all of which provided important indoor spaces to the Committee. These large public buildings soon served as hospitals, food storage and distribution points, administrative centers, and occasional refuges for the most vulnerable people to seek sanctuary inside the Safety Zone.

Luckily, missionary work and business experience gave the odd assemblage of foreigners on the International Committee the drive and organizational ability necessary to put together a massive, if basic, rescue scheme on a very tight schedule. Using university-educated Chinese as their lieutenants, the Committee members demarcated the Safety Zone's boundaries with numerous flags, many laid flat on rooftops or the ground so that Japanese airmen could clearly see the Zone's edges.

Helpers put up posters in Chinese throughout the city, urging residents and refugees alike to gather inside the Safety Zone. This soon produced a flood of thousands of people trying to find safety for themselves and their families. The organizers sent their limited supply of trucks throughout the city, collecting rice and other food stores abandoned by the Chinese military, along with medicine and other vital supplies.

The International Committee also contacted the headquarters of the Japanese 10th Army and requested that the soldiers of the Empire of Japan refrain from shelling or bombing the Zone. The Japanese, mostly because they wished to avoid killing foreigners and thus turn the western powers against them, agreed, and largely respected this agreement. However, the Safety Zone eventually proved somewhat less safe than hoped.

John Rabe had only slight faith in the Japanese promises not to shell the Zone. However, with characteristic humor, he took advantage of his own fears to include a wryly jocular entry in his diary on December 11th, referencing his pet bird, Peter: "Water and electricity are off. The bombardment continues. Now and then the noise ebbs a bit, only to break out anew. Our Peter appears to love it. He sings along at full throat. Canaries apparently have better nerves than a Rabe." (Rabe, 1998, 60).

Despite the Committee's efforts to disarm them or clear them out entirely, armed Chinese soldiers from the Nationalist forces remained inside the Safety Zone. Their presence caused immense alarm to the organizers, who feared the Japanese would simply launch a full-scale military attack and mow down everyone in their attempt to kill the soldiers using the Zone as "cover." However, they still expected the Japanese to behave in accordance with the laws of war and the Safety Zone to be needed only briefly. The first entry of Japanese troops into Nanking disabused them of these high-flown expectations abruptly and shockingly.

Chapter 6: The Arrival of the Japanese

The sound of gunfire accompanied the entry of the Japanese into Nanking – not the back-and-forth exchange of firefights between attackers and defenders, since the Chinese soldiery no longer resisted at that point, but the slowly spreading discharges of death squads mowing down randomly encountered people in the streets.

When the Japanese moved forward to take the metropolis, some of the half-million resident Chinese remaining within its walls actually ran out the gates to welcome them. They met with a very different reception than they expected from the victorious Imperial Japanese Army (IJA). Estimates put the number of people shot within the first two days of Nanking's fall at between 7,000 and 12,000, most gunned down casually by troops moving to take up positions assigned to them in the city's districts.

Eyewitnesses reported seeing many corpses lying along the streets with gunshot wounds in their backs as people, realizing the nature of their new masters, vainly attempted to flee the men Chiang Kai-Shek characterized as "dwarf bandits." The vanguard consisted of the 6th and 116th Infantry Divisions, supported by the 16th Division, which entered via the Taiping and Zhongshan Gates, and the 9th Division, marching through the Guanghua Gate.

While the Japanese initially avoided mass murder inside the Safety Zone, soldiers entered it almost immediately to loot and commit rape. Even in the first few days, some Chinese men in the Zone died to IJA bullets when they attempted to keep their wives, sisters, or daughters from suffering rape. Lewis Smythe, Secretary of the International Committee, wrote a long list of grievances to Japanese command, including this item:

> "On the night of December 14, there were many cases of Japanese soldiers entering Chinese houses and raping women or taking them away. This created a panic in the area and hundreds of women moved into the Ginling College campus yesterday. Consequently, three American men spent the night at Ginling College last night to protect the 3,000 women and children in the compound." (Brook, 1999, 10).

These actions – including random bayoneting and shooting of Chinese men – created an immediate crisis. Many of the Committee's Chinese helpers refused to go outside to prepare and distribute rice to the refugees, fearing murder by the prowling Japanese. With just 27 foreigners – able to move freely without risk of attack – in total, feeding thousands of refugees immediately grew into an insurmountable problem.

Predictably, worse soon followed. To provide some security for the Safety Zone, the International Committee organized Chinese volunteers into a temporary, unarmed police force. The Japanese targeted these men next, as John Rabe explained in a polite but deeply indignant letter to the IJA command on December 17th:

"Our police were interfered with and yesterday 50 of them stationed at the Ministry of Justice were marched off, 'to be killed' according to the Japanese officer in charge, and yesterday afternoon 46 of our 'volunteer police' were similarly marched off. [...] These 'volunteer police' were neither uniformed nor armed in any way. They simply wore our armbands. They were more like Boy Scouts in the West who do odd jobs in helping to keep crowds in order, clean up, and render first aid, etc." (Brook, 1999, 14).

Trying to keep their charges alive, the westerners of the International Committee used the private cars at their disposal to distribute as much food as possible to the Chinese cowering indoors, fearing to emerge into the streets where Japanese soldiers prowled, looking for items to steal and women to rape.

General Matsui Iwane, the 10th Army commander, only entered the city on December 17th, riding on horseback and accompanied by an escorting unit of cavalry for his grand entrance. Matsui remained for only five days before returning to Shanghai on December 22nd, 1937.

Matsui Iwane

The general later sanctimoniously claimed ignorance of the incident, while simultaneously and rather contradictorily asserting he dressed down Prince Akaga and other field commanders for "abominable incidents" lasting "50 days" in Nanking. This, of course, begs the question why Matsui, if truly as outraged as he claimed, failed to return even once to Nanking to halt the massacre, or even attempt to halt it.

Even if Matsui did, in fact, verbally assail his subordinates over the ongoing slaughter and mass rape, he never issued a written order to stop or even condemn it. His admission that he knew of the Rape of Nanking and his indisputable inaction (at the very least) in failing to deal with it sufficed for the Allied war crimes judges after the war, who sentenced him to hang.

Though the Japanese soldiers began an orgy of looting, rape, torture, and mass murder immediately after their arrival, they did not run amok in the usual understanding of the word. They remained highly organized, showing that military discipline and chain of command still operated to the full. In fact, many of the atrocities could not have occurred without large-scale coordination and careful planning, enabling the efficient movement of large numbers of prisoners to killing sites, the disposal of bodies, and so on.

Even more starkly, the immunity enjoyed by the tiny handful of Americans, Germans, and other European foreigners amid the khaki ocean of the Japanese 10th Army demonstrates incontrovertibly that the chain of command remained intact and the officer corps maintained iron control throughout the Massacre. The members of the International Committee photographed and filmed the horrors taking place, berated and harassed Japanese soldiers engaged in war crimes, and sometimes even physically intervened to prevent rapes. Yet not one died, or even suffered a wound, at the hands of the soldiers.

This is not to say the Japanese soldiers participated unwillingly. On the contrary, most appeared eager to let loose the inmost appetites of the human animal. In the words of one Japanese medical corps Staff Sergeant, "The soldiers practically fell over themselves rushing to gang rape [the women]" (Honda, 2015, 120). However, those appetites, aggressions, and impulses operated only within precise boundaries set by the military authorities, and the survival of the meddling, isolated band of 27 foreigners in their midst through the whole six weeks of incessant slaughter underlines how scrupulously every soldier stayed within those boundaries, set by higher authority.

These facts strongly belie later claims by the Japanese officers that they lost control over their men and had no ability whatsoever to influence events. In fact, both officers and soldiers wanted precisely the same thing, and each cooperated fully in their role in carrying out what stands as probably history's largest single-location war crime.

Chapter 7: The Rape of Nanking

The Japanese carried out wholesale extermination attempts on the male population of

Nanking, likely killing well over 200,000 men in total. Most of these victims consisted of civilians, though prisoners of war and unarmed military deserters trying to hide in the local population also suffered destruction. A Japanese woman attached to a "Pacification Unit" later wrote about one of the many techniques used to kill men in large numbers:

> "Both men and women were stripped naked and made to march single file. The Japanese soldiers assembled on each side of the road, applauding and having a great time as they watched. The men were driven into the river, and as each one's head broke through to the water's surface, he was shot and killed right there. It's not hard to imagine how the remaining women were treated." (Honda, 2015, 121).

Shooting men in the Yangtze River solved the problem of corpse disposal also, since the stream carried away most of the cadavers. However, this represented only one of the many methods the IJA soldiery used in committing mass murder, as documented in excruciating detail both by foreign eyewitnesses and by numerous accounts and photographs generated by the Japanese themselves.

In some areas, the Japanese engaged in "beheading training," using samurai swords and other bladed weapons to sever the necks of numerous Chinese men. These massacres took place systematically next to huge open pits dug beforehand to receive the corpses. The Japanese roped the Chinese men together in long rows, then moved systematically down the line, chopping off heads and rolling the corpses into the mass graves.

Some Chinese escaped death when the Japanese, exhausted by the hard physical work of butchering thousands of human beings, substituted stabbing for decapitation. This allowed a few Chinese to throw themselves into the pit and sham death until the Japanese left, then crawl out and escape, fleeing into the countryside or to the Safety Zone.

Japanese Soldiers Searching Chinese for Weapons

    The Japanese also used tens of thousands of Chinese men for live bayonet practice. The soldiers forced Chinese to dig wide, shallow ditches, then herded their victims into the ditch with their hands pinioned behind their backs. Japanese soldiers carrying rifles with fixed bayonets then entered the ditch and practiced various close combat attacks on their helpless prisoners.

    Photographs of these scenes survive. In one example, the photographer captured the moment when one Japanese soldier stabs a man who is apparently sinking down and dying. A second Japanese jabs his bayonet into the abdomen of a prone form, apparently already dead or nearly so. In the foreground, a third IJA soldier is making a violent underarm thrust at a man curled up defensively against the wall of the trench, trying vainly to fend off the bayonet with his bare foot.

    Other Chinese died even more slowly. The Japanese bound groups of men hand and foot and buried them alive. In other cases, they buried the victims up to their necks, then ran their heads over with tanks or armored cars. In several cases, seeking sadistic entertainment, IJA soldiers buried groups of naked Chinese men up to their waists in the ground and then loosed attack-trained German shepherds on the victims. Half-buried, the men could not escape, but with their arms still free, they could attempt – vainly – to fend off the dogs, which ripped out their throats or disemboweled them.

In other cases, the Japanese soaked crowds of bound men in gasoline and either set them afire directly or shot them with machine guns, the tracer rounds setting the gasoline alight. So many corpses were collected that disposal became a massive problem, and the air filled with an overwhelming stench of decaying flesh even in winter. Photographs show heaps of dead bodies on the Yangtze shore and giant mass graves. Once the river froze over, the Japanese trucked corpses out onto the ice, cut large holes in the surface, and dumped their ghastly cargo through to be swept away downstream.

Thousands of other men died individually in casual killings or, very frequently, when they tried to defend their families from rape. Murder of a household's male inhabitants often served as a prelude to gang-rapes of its women. A few Japanese even reportedly cut off and ate the penises of Chinese men they killed, believing this would increase their sexual prowess and overall virility.

In other cases, the Japanese kept victims alive for extended torture. Soon after the occupation began, the soldiers stripped hundreds of men and women naked, tied them to the pillars in a university building, and probed their bodies with sharpened awls, inflicting hundreds of wounds on each. A number of observers, both foreign and Chinese, reported on incidents where the Japanese suspended prisoners – both men and women – by hooks driven through their tongues, then watched the agonized struggles of the victims.

Some of the Japanese expressed shock and amazement when first confronted by the outpouring of violence. One officer named Tominaga Shozo, arriving on the scene fresh from the academy, felt a measure of alarm when he first got a close look at the men the Army assigned him to command: "They had evil eyes," he remembered. "They weren't human eyes, but the eyes of leopards or tigers." (Chang, 1997, 48).

Officers made sure to harden such men to killing quickly by ordering them to bayonet or behead terrified prisoners. Many, already fully indoctrinated by the militaristic culture and a contempt for their own lives that made them value those of other people even less, adapted almost instantly to the grisly sport. While Tominaga Shozo stated it took three months for him to become a "demon," other men like Nagatomi Hakudo readily admitted to exulting in killing almost from the first:

"The Japanese officer [...] unsheathed his sword, spat on it, and with a sudden mighty swing he brought it down on the neck of a Chinese boy cowering before us. The head was cut clean off and tumbled away [...] as the body slumped forward, blood spurting in two great gushing fountains from the neck. The officer suggested I take the head home as a souvenir. I remember smiling proudly as I took his sword and began killing people." (Chang, 1997, 49).

Nagatomi, never punished for his crimes, later became a doctor and, when asked, stated that he murdered approximately 200 prisoners personally during his time in Nanking, using beheading, live burial, and burning alive. While the Japanese killed the largest portion of the men in the first week or two of occupation, thousands more murders and executions – often carried out in extremely torturous fashion – continued throughout the entire six-week period of the Massacre.

Amid a sea of slaughter so vast its perpetrators frequently blend into an anonymous, bloodthirsty collective, at least one incident stands out sharply as the handiwork of two identifiable individuals. The so-called "Contest to Cut Down a Hundred" between two second lieutenants appeared in a series of articles printed in the Tokyo Nichinichi Shimbun newspaper in late 1937, detailing the supposed "heroic" deeds of the "contestants."

Noda Tsuyoshi and Mukai Toshiaki, two second lieutenants, began a "contest" to see who could kill 100 Chinese first. The newspapers reported the grisly affair as occurring in the thick of battle:

"As Second Lieutenant M[ukai], who has reached the third *dan* in bayonet training, runs his fingers over the blade of "Seki-no-Magoroku," the sword at his side, Second Lieutenant N[oda] speaks of his treasured sword […] On the day after their separate departures, Second Lieutenant N[oda] broke into an enemy pillbox [and] killed four enemy […] Second Lieutenant M[ukai] invaded an enemy camp at Henglinzhen […] and laid fifty-five enemy low with his sword." (Honda, 2015, 125).

A Japanese Story Describing the "Contest"

    The incident highlights the incredible levels of jingoism inculcated into the Japanese of the era by their government, and the underdevelopment of critical thinking skills even in those otherwise well-educated by Imperial universities. Most Japanese interpreted the contest as meaning the second lieutenants charged heroically in amongst the Chinese enemy and cut down dozens like action movie samurai.

    No such action could in fact occur. The Nationalist soldiers, well-armed with high powered rifles generally maintained better than their owners, would inevitably have killed a lone man with a sword attempting to close to melee range. Even if trained to standards inferior to those used for Japanese soldiers, the idea of a swordsman plowing through trenches or camps filled with hostile riflemen and leaving "red ruin" in his wake appears ludicrous and impossible.

Noda himself scoffed at the notion when he spoke at the school in his hometown and frankly admitted to committing mass murder of helpless prisoners. After declaring "that stuff in the newspapers about the 'brave warrior from the provinces' and the 'brave warrior of contest to cut down a hundred,' that's me," he described how once a band of Chinese soldiers surrendered to the Japanese:

"We'd line them up and cut them down, from one end of the line to the other. I was praised for having killed a hundred people, but actually, almost all of them were killed in this way. The two of us did have a contest, but afterward, I was often asked whether it was a big deal, and I said that it was no big deal." (Honda, 2015, 126).

The heroism, in fact, consisted of plain butchery. Since both men passed 100 "kills" and remained uncertain who "scored" the highest first, they went into what the newspapers called "extra innings" to see who could reach 150 first.

The newspaper clippings later proved the two officers' doom. Presented at trial as evidence of war crimes, the articles assured Mukai's and Noda's condemnation to death, a verdict greeted by a round of spontaneous, enthusiastic applause in the Chinese postwar courtroom. The Chinese executed the two lieutenants by firing squad.

Accompanying the endless scenes of butchery that choked every street and alley in the city with bloated, reeking corpses, the Japanese raped nearly every woman they could catch. While naturally giving preference to young, attractive women, the soldiers raped females of every age, including the very old and the very young. The IJA soldiery raped at least 80,000 women. Many of these unfortunates suffered violation dozens of times. In a number of cases, so many men raped women in succession that they ruptured the women's genital area in the process, causing them to bleed to death.

The Japanese soldiers usually killed any men present before or after the rapes, particularly if the Chinese dared to attempt fighting off the rapists, who typically moved in bands of 20 to 30 to ensure their ability to overwhelm any opposition. At other times, however, the IJA soldiers amused themselves by forcing men to rape their relatives, such as making fathers rape their daughters or sons rape their mothers while the Japanese watched. Many Chinese refused, resulting in their immediate murder by the troops. At least one family committed mass suicide by leaping into the Yangtze and drowning rather than submit to raping one another.

While most rapes involved men raping women, some of the Japanese soldiers also raped Chinese men. A variant on the theme involved forcing Chinese men to rape each other under threat of immediate execution in the case of non-compliance. The Japanese also sodomized men with foreign objects, often inflicting fatal injuries in the process.

When the rapes usually ended with the murder of the women involved. Frequently, the killing of the women involved the most gruesome kinds of torture. A favorite method of executing a rape victim involved shoving a long sharpened bamboo stake, a cane, a bayonet, or another sharp foreign object into her vagina, causing her to die from internal injuries. Several photographs of female bodies in this condition survive, in one case with a Japanese soldier standing calmly next to the corpse.

In other cases, the soldiers stuffed live grenades or lit firecrackers into the victim's vagina to kill her. Many others simply died under a flurry of bayonet thrusts or received the relative mercy of shooting. However, the soldiers often seemed to be on the lookout for sadistic ways to increase their victim's suffering with an agonizing death following the shock and horror of violation, as a medical officer later confessed:

"There was a girl – she may have waited too long to flee – who had blackened her face and put on men's clothes and waded into the river to hide. The soldiers pulled her out of the river and made her rinse herself off... The way it ended was that they tied her hands, shoved her into a shed that had straw piled up around it, and burned her to death." (Honda, 2015, 120).

The Japanese raped female children and sometimes infants also. If the act proved impossible initially for physical reasons, the soldiers simply sliced the victim's genital area open with a bayonet before committing the rape. Frequently, soldiers killed a woman's child first before raping her. Others slashed open the stomachs of pregnant women and extracted the fetuses to kill separately before leaving the woman to die of her injuries. One Japanese sergeant later left a harrowing account:

"I took a living human child, that is, an innocent baby that was just beginning to talk, and threw it into boiling water. When the mother, desperate to save her child, rushed over to the kettle, I sneered contemptuously and said, 'If you take care of the brat, you'll be next, and I'll do it slowly.' Then I kicked her in the abdomen so she went flying." (Honda, 2015, 121).

Other women became sex slaves for the conquering Japanese, their degradation continuing for the entire period of the Massacre or in some cases longer. At the bottom of this ghastly hierarchy of victims existed women turned into a sort of "rape furniture," tied naked to posts or bed frames at the entrances to barracks or inside the barracks themselves. Left in these exposed positions for extended periods of time, these women remained available for casual rape by any passing Japanese who randomly felt the urge to violate them. Once damaged or otherwise rendered less attractive, the Japanese often killed them and replaced them with other victims.

The Japanese soldiers also objected to washing their own garments, so the Army gathered large numbers of women to serve as laundry slaves. Kept prisoner near barracks and other facilities, these women scrubbed uniforms clean by day, then suffered sexual assault at night for the entertainment of their captors. As a letter from Dr. Robert O. Wilson of the University

Hospital, an American, to the Japanese authorities described, speaking of one such incident:

"They were taken by Japanese soldiers to a location in the west central portion of the city where from the activity she judged there was a Japanese military hospital. The women washed clothes during the day and were raped throughout the night. The older ones were being raped from 10 to 20 times, the younger and good looking ones as many as 40 times a night." (Brook, 1999, 65).

The Japanese forced the most attractive women into service as "comfort women" in early examples of their infamous "comfort stations." Though generally not raped to death, and very seldom bayoneted or shot, these women remained as sexual captives for years – permanent slaves meant to satisfy the lusts of Japanese soldiers stationed in the city or moving through it on their way to other postings.

Those women not killed outright during or immediately after rape often found themselves pregnant with a half-Japanese child. Many women killed these infants immediately after their birth. Others, when they realized their pregnancy, committed suicide by leaping from rooftops or drowning themselves in the Yangtze, joining those who killed themselves due to being unable to cope with the emotional devastation following sexual assault. A few carried their babies to term and then raised them, but often remained conflicted and tormented for years about their choice.

Though hampered by their low numbers and lack of any effective power beyond that offered by courage and a sense of moral duty, the foreign members of the International Committee for the Safety Zone did their best to ameliorate the horrors around them. When they could not, they used still cameras and, in the case of the missionary John Magee, an early motion picture camera, to document as much of the mayhem and slaughter as possible for eventual war crimes prosecution.

The Committee members worked hard to keep people inside the Safety Zone safe from execution or kidnapping. They also sought to prevent rapes, though the Japanese frequently broke into houses or dormitories at night and raped dozens of women anyway. Using the medical supplies gathered, they treated hundreds of victims with bayonet or bullet wounds, sword wounds, or genitals mangled by mass gang-rape. They also kept thousands alive by organizing relief kitchens and providing rice meals on a daily basis, sometimes supplemented with fish or chicken when they could buy these meats.

Medical care and food – often prepared and distributed by Chinese assistants to John Rabe's "Red Swastika" branch, the Nazi equivalent of the Red Cross – accounted for most of the help the Committee could provide to the people of Nanking. By their count, approximately 49,000 to 51,000 people sheltered inside the Safety Zone. While not immune to rape and murder, these individuals experienced less violence than those in the city and its suburbs, and received regular food from the huge kitchens organized by the missionaries, doctors, and businesspeople.

These individuals at least owed their survival mainly to the International Committee, due to immense food scarcity in the city.

These brave men and women also protested constantly – though futility – to the Japanese authorities, sending countless letters describing rape, pillage, and murder. Courteously but insistently, they demanded redress, though of course the IJA made no effort to oblige.

On some occasions, the foreigners managed to intervene in an individual rape or killing and save the victim. They could do nothing, of course, for those rounded up for mass torture and execution, where thousands of Japanese soldiers acted in concert under the command of their officers. John Rabe managed on several occasions to overawe potential rapists by displaying the emblem of Nazi Germany, Japan's ally:

> "Six Japanese climbed over my garden wall and attempted to open the gates from the inside. When I arrive and shine my flashlight in the face of one of the bandits, he reaches for his pistol, but his hand drops quickly enough when I yell at him and hold my swastika armband under his nose. Then, on my orders, all six have to scramble back over the wall. My gates will never be opened to riffraff like that " (Rabe, 1998, 34).

The Japanese excluded other foreigners from entering the city also. Diplomatic representatives of America and Germany naturally wished to learn the fate and situation of their citizens in Nanking, but the IJA maintained close control on all movements into and out of the city, as noted in the diary of Tsen Shui-Feng, the Chinese assistant of Minnie Vautrin, a missionary who undertook organizing the protection, feeding, and medical treatment of women and children in the Safety Zone:

> "The Americans requested the Japanese consul to telegram Shanghai for more manpower to help here. They refused. They deliberately did so. The German consul at Hsia Kwan is not allowed to enter the city [...] He [the Japanese consul] wants neither the third country [Germany] to see their immoral deeds, nor people to see the corpses lying on the roads. Some of the roads, [people] can only see dead bodies, but not the road." (Hu, 2010, 99).

The Japanese refused to allow additional foreigners to enter the city until the spring of 1938, by which time they concealed much of the evidence of massacre through burial and cremation. During the worst of the mayhem, a news blackout by the Imperial occupiers effectively concealed the extent and savagery of the destruction from the outside world.

After the first month of terror and destruction, the Rape of Nanking's fury slowly ebbed. Murder, torture, rape, looting, and arson continued well into January 1938, but at a declining rate. Miner Searle Bates, a university historian, highlighted the reason for this in a letter sent to unspecified acquaintances in the United States:

"Dear Friends: – A few hasty jottings amid rape and bayonet stabs and reckless shooting, to be sent on the first foreign boat available since the situation developed after the Japanese entry – a U.S. Navy tug [...] Things have eased a good deal since New Year within the crowded Safety Zone, largely through the departure of the main hordes of soldiers." (Kaiyuan, 2001, 14).

The behavior of the Japanese soldiers underwent little change but their numbers dwindled as the Tenth Army shifted south for new campaigns (and brought massacre and mass rape to new towns, villages, and regions). On January 1st, 1938, the Japanese established a puppet government made up of Chinese under Japanese military authority, the Nanjing Zizhi Weiyuanhui, or Nanking Self-Government Committee.

The new Chinese government proved a mixed blessing. The officials themselves lost no time in enrichment through plunder, adding to the problems of a city already picked clean with vulture-like efficiency by the Japanese. However, they also did much to restore the metropolis to some sort of working order. The deep drifts of garbage and shredded, putrid human flesh which the Japanese left in the roads, killing anyone who dared to attempt cleanup, now underwent removal under the Zizhi Weiyuanhui's supervision.

Within a month, the city once again enjoyed electricity, running water, and ricksha and bus services. The stench of death lingered but slowly abated. The Japanese, whose garrison ceased random killings once the Tenth Army left, established shops to exploit the population (whose own stores the Japanese earlier destroyed systematically), and built opium dens throughout the city. The misery of their situation prompted people to grasp at the brief respite drugs offered: "To encourage addiction and further enslave the people, the Japanese routinely used narcotics as payment for labor and prostitution in Nanking. Heroin cigarettes were offered to children as young as ten. Based on his research [...] Miner Searle Bates concluded that some fifty thousand people in the Nanking area were using heroin— one-eighth of the population at the time."

Chinese workers in Japanese factories received pay but also suffered frequent abuse, up to and including execution by torture for minor thefts. The infamous Unit 731, which carried out lethal medical experiments on living human beings, opened a heavily guarded facility in Nanking. Here, anyone accused of minor infractions against Japanese regulations might find themselves dissected alive, infected with fatal disease organisms and left untreated, or subjected to a range of agonizing, grotesque medical experiments, before being dumped into the facility's incinerator.

Nevertheless, Nanking rebounded once massacre and random killing in the streets ceased. Though oppressed and tormented for the remainder of the war, the Chinese population of the city managed to restore a semblance of normal life and carry on agricultural and economic activity, a striking testament to human resiliency.

Chapter 8: Postwar Justice and War Crimes Trials

When the Japanese evacuated the city in 1945, following the American atomic bombing of Nagasaki and Hiroshima, very few reprisals occurred against them by the Chinese despite the defeat of the Empire of the Rising Sun. Thoroughly terrorized and cowed by Japanese brutality, the Chinese mostly hid themselves in their houses for several days, emerging to find the streets finally empty of the hated ocher uniforms of Japan.

The number of people killed during the Rape of Nanking remains under dispute to this day. Japanese nationalist revisionists, flying in the face of overwhelming evidence – including Japanese photographs and the testimony and memoirs of numerous IJA personnel – attempt to declare the number as low as 40,000, or even 10,000.

Though the Japanese destroyed many of their military documents relating to Nanking, and others remain classified by the Japanese government, detailed burial records and Japanese corpse disposal records indicate a minimum of 219,000 victims, of whom 76% consisted of men, 22% of women, and 2% of children of both sexes. Such estimates provide a conservative baseline, considering that the Japanese dumped thousands of bodies in the Yangtze to be carried away and thoroughly cremated thousands of others.

An overall estimate of 250,000 dead appears reasonable, with up to 300,000 possible. Both the United States and the Chinese held war crimes trials for some of the leading perpetrators, though most ordinary soldiers who killed, tortured, and raped men, women, and children escaped any kind of justice and returned quietly to private life.

In sentencing, the International Military Tribunal for the Far East cited a statement issued by Matsui Iwane on October 8th, 1937, containing the typical swaggering braggadocio of IJA pronouncements and indicating his complicity in all of the ensuing slaughters visited on the Chinese:

> "The devil-defying sharp bayonets were just on the point of being unsheathed so as to develop their divine influence, and that the mission of the Army was to fulfill all its duties of protecting Japanese residents and interests, and to chastise the Nanking government and the outrageous Chinese." (Brook, 1999, 257).

Matsui Iwane proved slippery and evasive in the witness stand, changing his story repeatedly, sometimes fully acknowledging the horrors committed and revealing some unknown to the Tribunal until that time, at others denying that the Japanese killed or raped anyone in Nanking. He also alternately accepted responsibility and claimed total ignorance of events. His only firm stance centered on deflecting all blame from the Imperial family, even though much evidence pointed to the culpability of Prince Asaka Yasuhiko, who also proved instrumental in the IJA's abandonment of international law.

General Douglas MacArthur, who paradoxically shielded Japanese war criminals, and in particular protected the Japanese imperial family from their obvious guilt in many of Japan's most heinous war crimes, granted immunity from prosecution to Prince Asaka. Matsui hanged, as did six other men. Eighteen more received lighter sentences. In all, the Allies executed only seven men in retribution for the 219,000 or more slaughtered in Nanking.

Douglas MacArthur

The Chinese executed four Imperial Japanese officers in their custody following the Nanjing War Crimes Tribunal organized by Chiang Kai-Shek. Of these, Tani Hisao drew the most opprobrium during his trial. Thousands of spectators arrived to watch the isolated figure in the defendants' dock and to listen to the endless litany of horrors recited by hundreds of survivors and other eyewitnesses. The prosecution even brought several mounds of bullet-punctured, blood-stained skulls into the courtroom, excavated from mass graves found beside Nanking's walls.

The court naturally found Tani Hisao guilty and, on April 26th, 1947, Chinese soldiers drove the pinioned general through the streets of Nanking along a route flanked by immense crowds, with a soldier named Tang Zeqi at the wheel. After his parade through the streets, his orders had helped fill with human blood and anguish, the Chinese led Tani to Rain Flower Terrace south of the city. The crowds roared "Revenge!" over and over as the defeated general passed among them.

Finally, at the terrace, a soldier who survived one of the Japanese massacres at Nanking approached Tani from behind and fired a pistol into his head at point blank range. The Chinese judges felt it appropriate that a man nearly killed by Tani's orders should perform the actual execution. A surviving photograph shows the moment of Tani Hisao's death, with the Japanese war criminal jerking forward, and the taller Chinese soldier firing a Hanyang C.96 7.62 mm pistol, copied from the Mauser C96, into his skull. A large crowd of Chinese spectators stands in the background.

As a somber footnote to the colossal Japanese war crime, the pioneering author of the first major book to bring the incident to western attention, Iris Shun-Ru Chang, committed suicide with a revolver near Los Gatos, California on November 9th, 2004. Deeply depressed and haunted by the horrors she researched, and subject to a bout of brief reactive psychosis, along with symptoms of PTSD, Ms. Chang tragically became the final victim of the Nanking Massacre, 67 years after the last shot was fired and the last samurai sword swung in the blood-stained ruins of the martyred city.

Online Resources

Other World War II titles by Charles River Editors

Other titles about the rape of Nanking on Amazon

Bibliography

Bix, Herbert P. Hirohito and the Making of Modern Japan. New York, 2000.

Brook, Timothy. Documents on the Rape of Nanking. Ann Arbor, 1999.

Chang, Iris. The Rape of Nanking: The Forgotten Holocaust of World War II. New York, 1997.

Hawley, Samuel. The Imjin War: Japan's Sixteenth Century Invasion of Korea and Attempt to Conquer China. London, 2005.

Honda Katsuichi. The Nanjing Massacre: A Japanese Journalist Confronts Japan's National Shame. New York, 2015.

Hu, Hua-ling, and Lian-Hong Zhang. The Undaunted Women of Nanking: The Wartime Diaries of Minnie Vautrin and Tsen Shui-Fang. Carbondale, 2010.

Kaiyuan, Zhang. Eyewitness to Massacre. Armonk, 2001.

Paine, S.C.M. The Wars for Asia, 1911-1949. New York, 2012.

Rabe, John. The Good Man of Nanking: The Diaries of John Rabe. New York, 1998.

Taylor, Jay. The Generalissimo: Chiang Kai-Shek and the Struggle for Modern China. Cambridge, 2009.

Turnbull, Stephen. Samurai Invasion: Japan's Korean War, 1592-1598. London, 2002.

Made in the USA
Monee, IL
09 April 2020